Real World

Colouring Book

For Advanced Users & Adults

50 Images

**Created From Real Life Photos
For You To Colour As You Please.**

ISBN 978-0-359-86478-2
90000
9 780359 864782

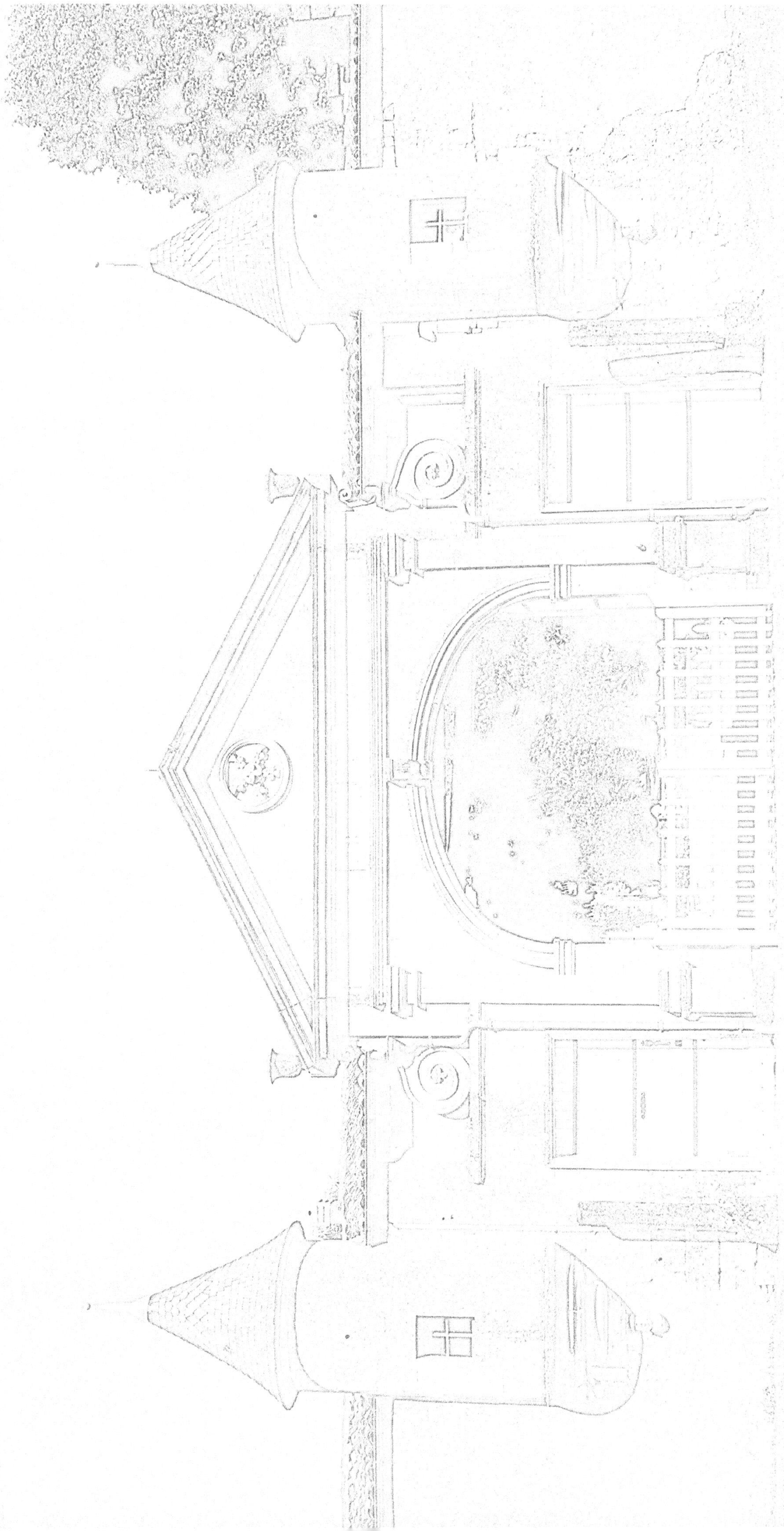

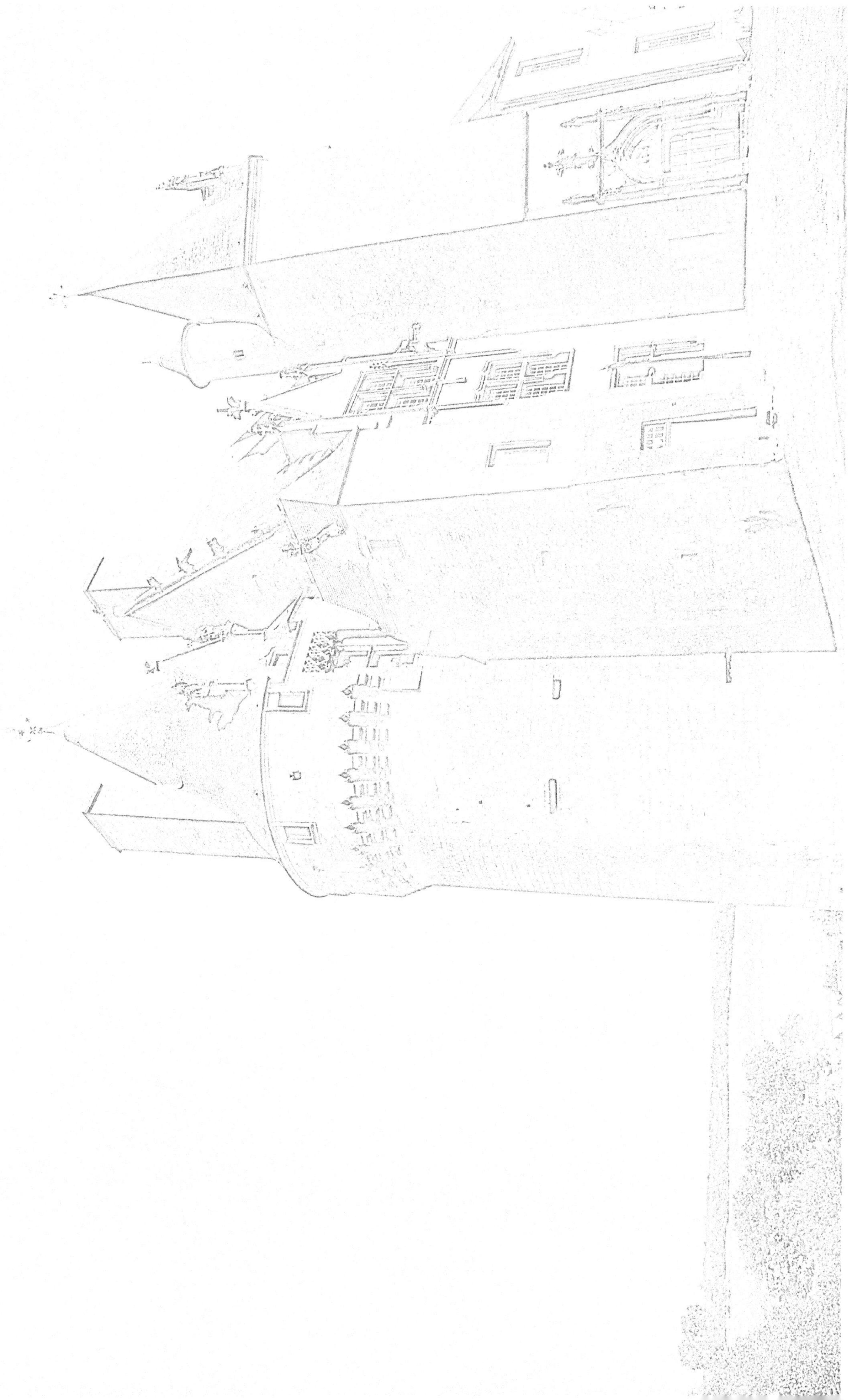

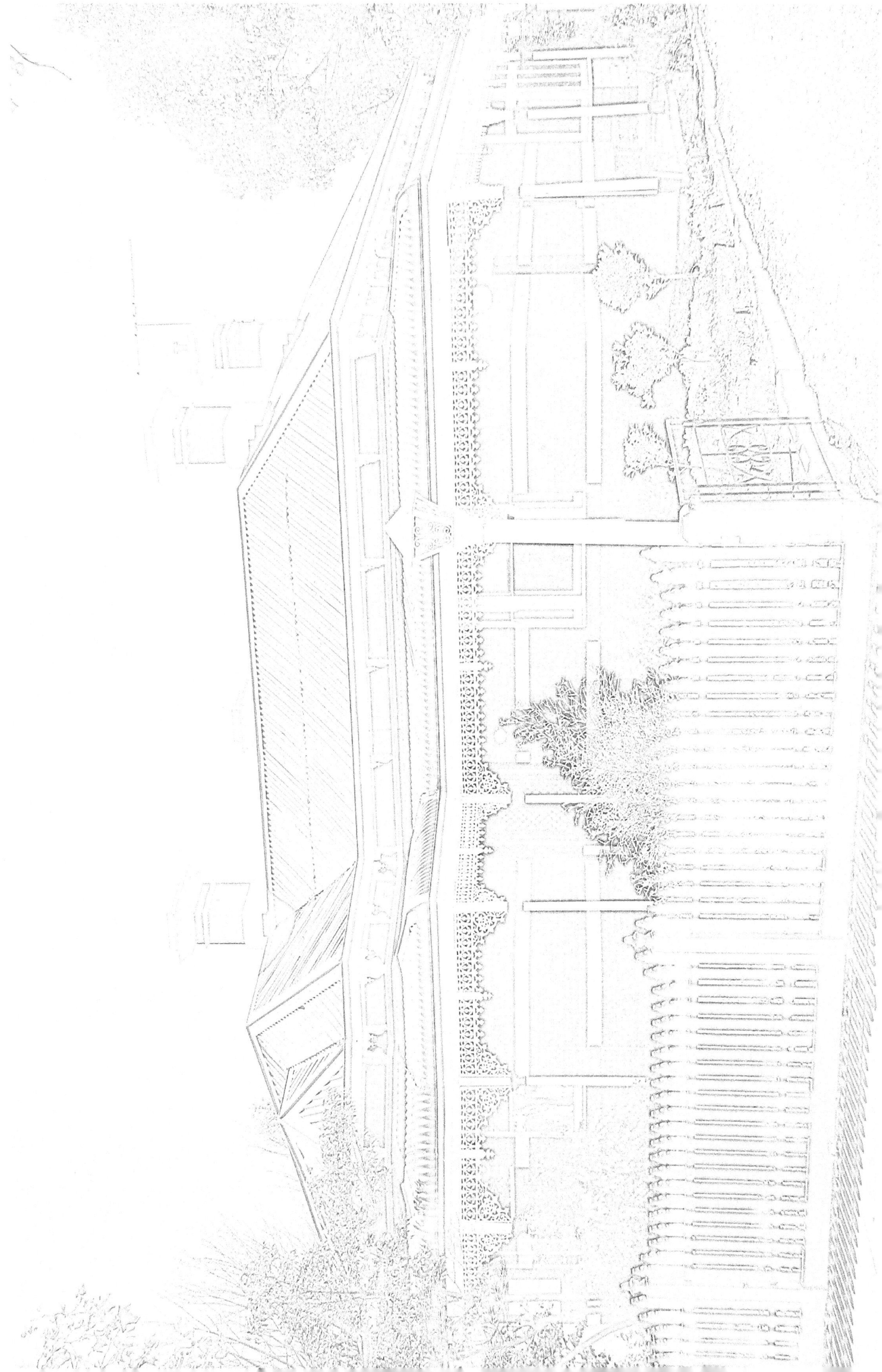

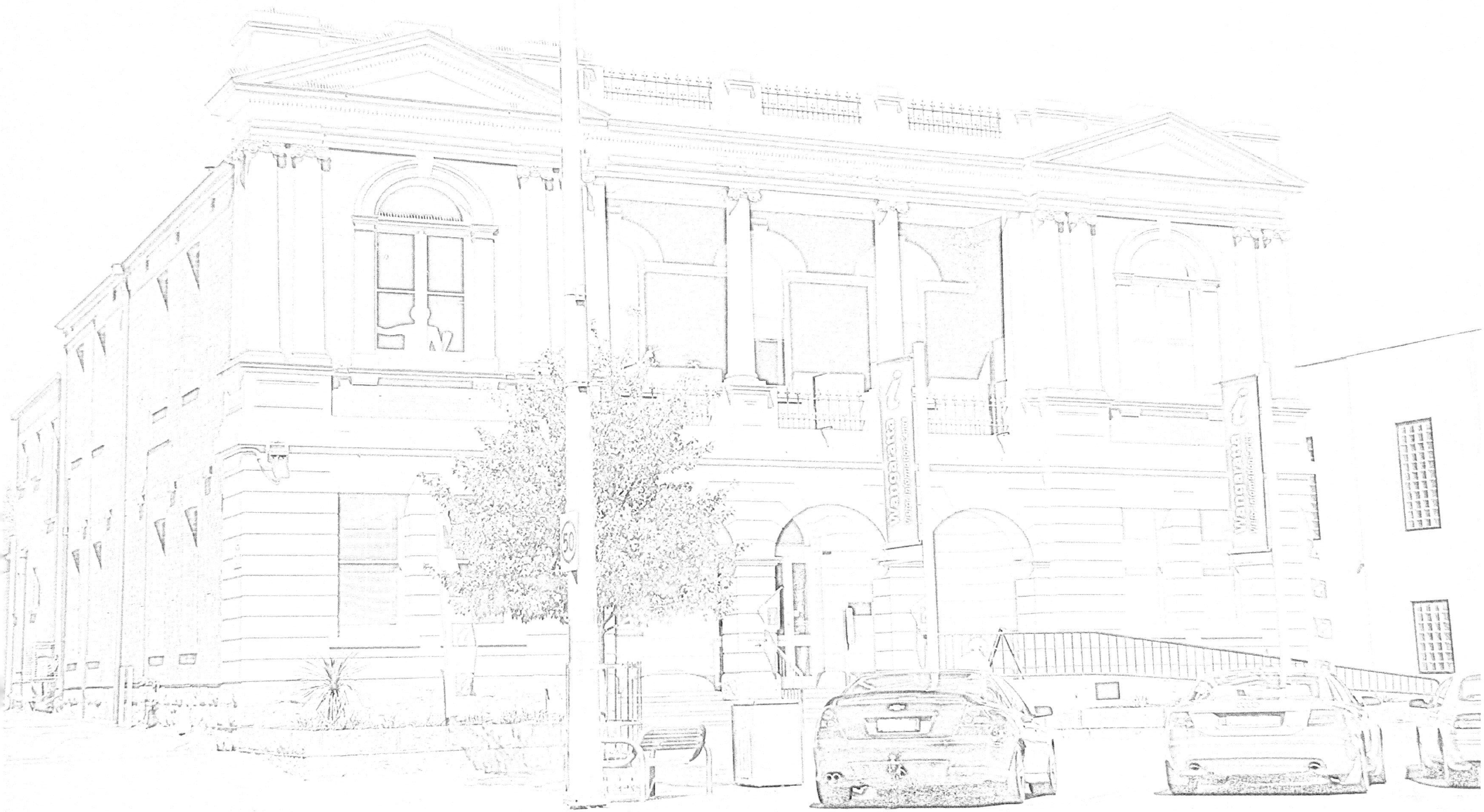
50

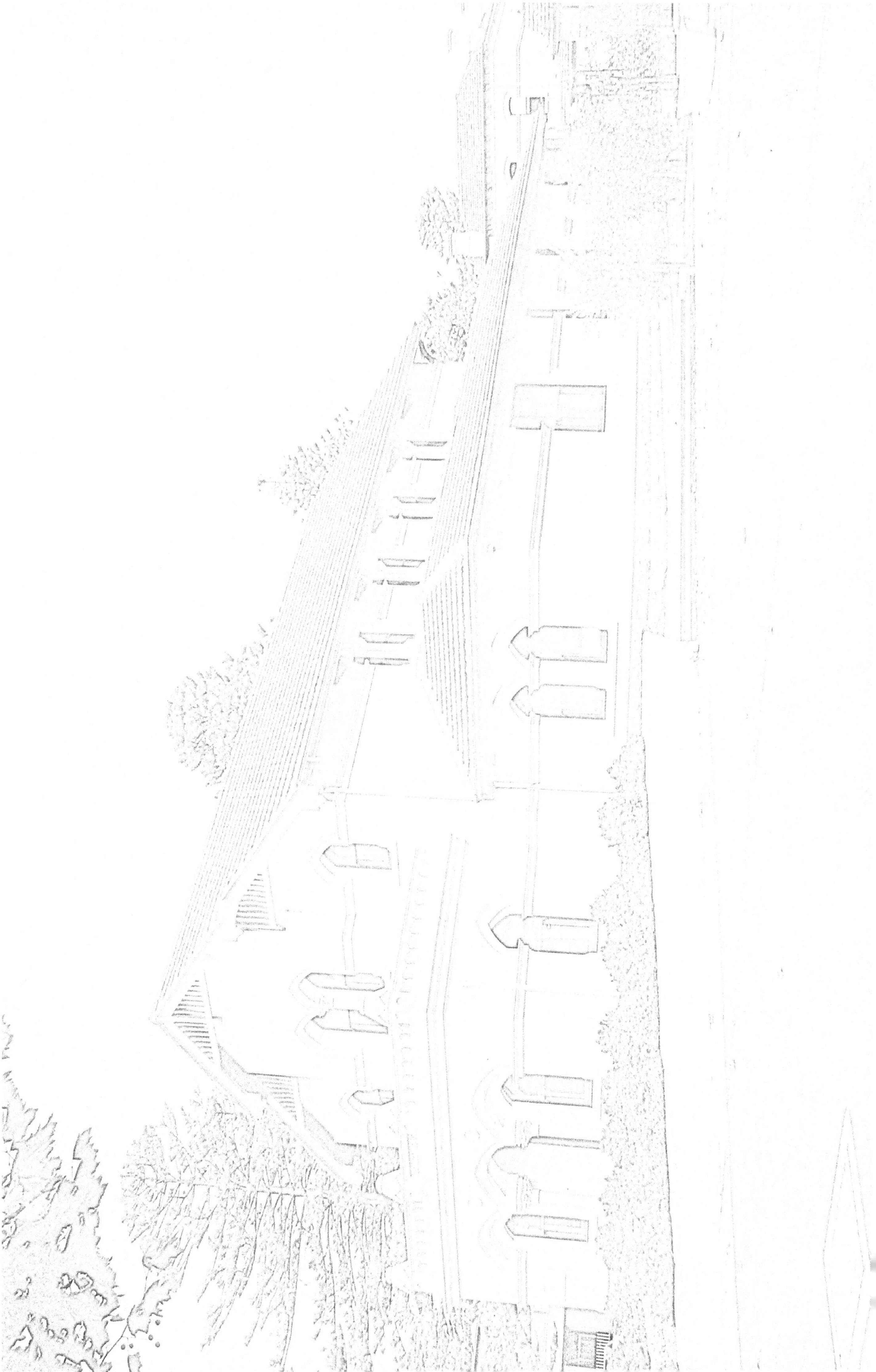

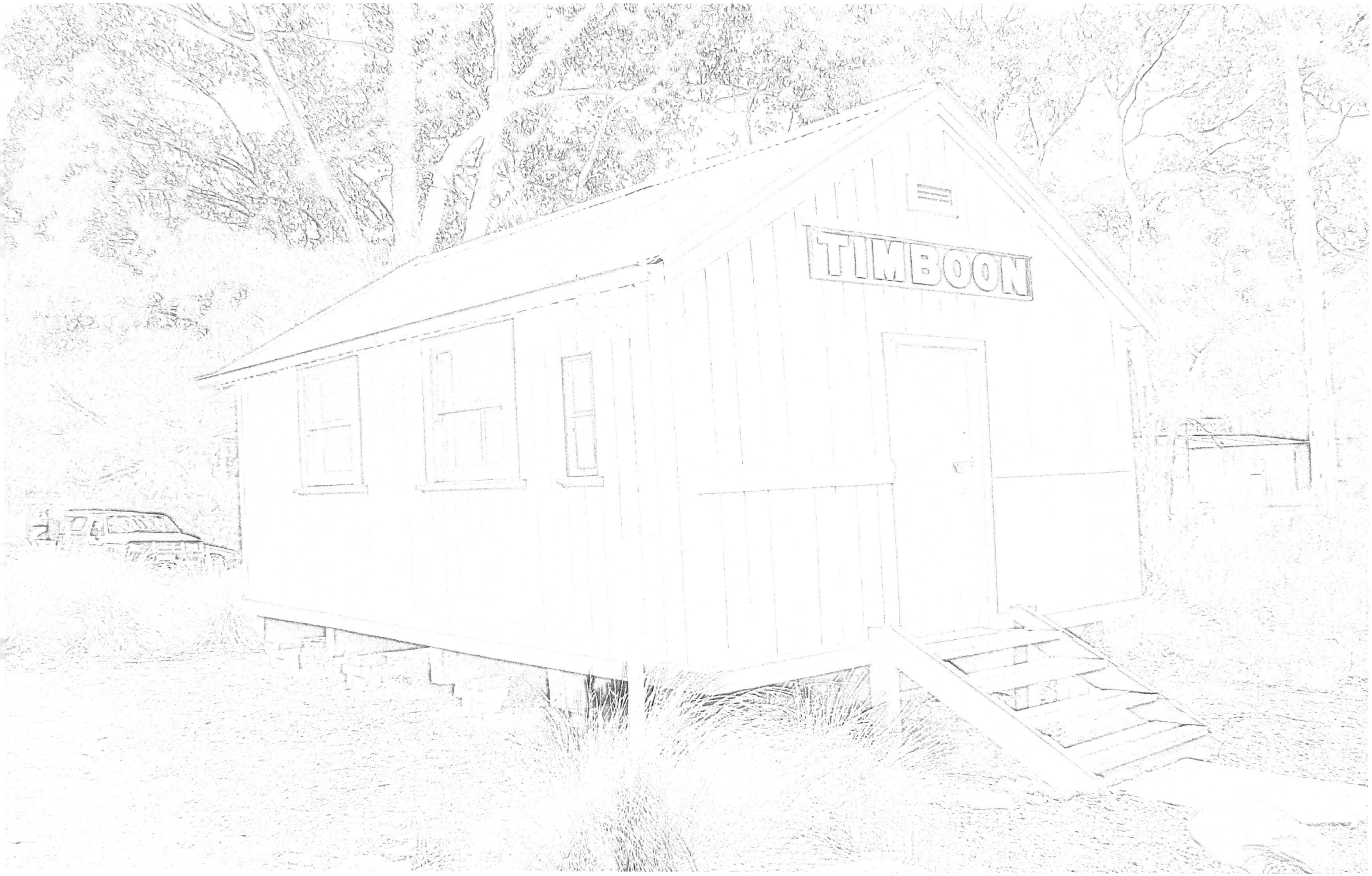
TIMBOON

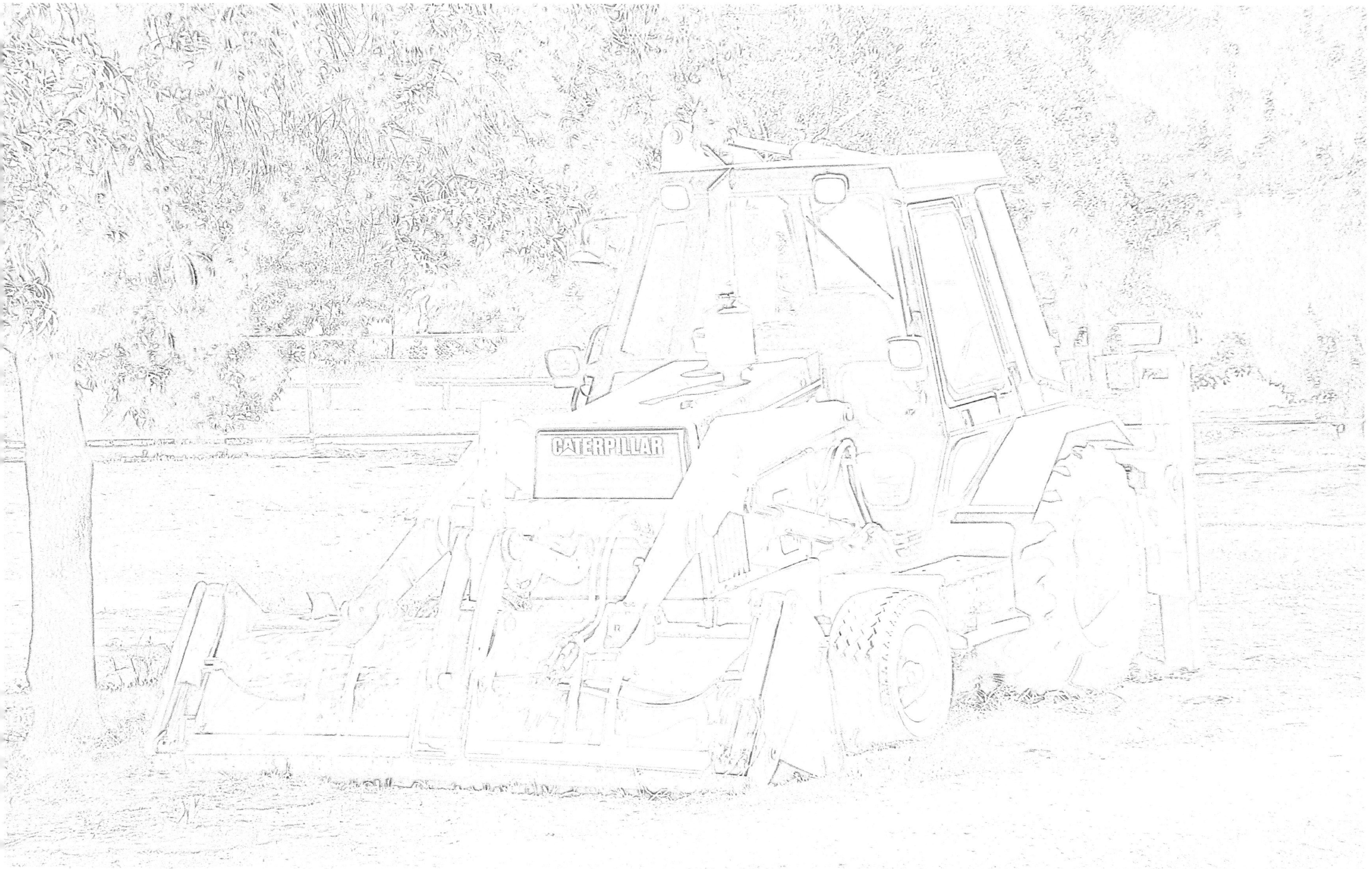
CATERPILLAR

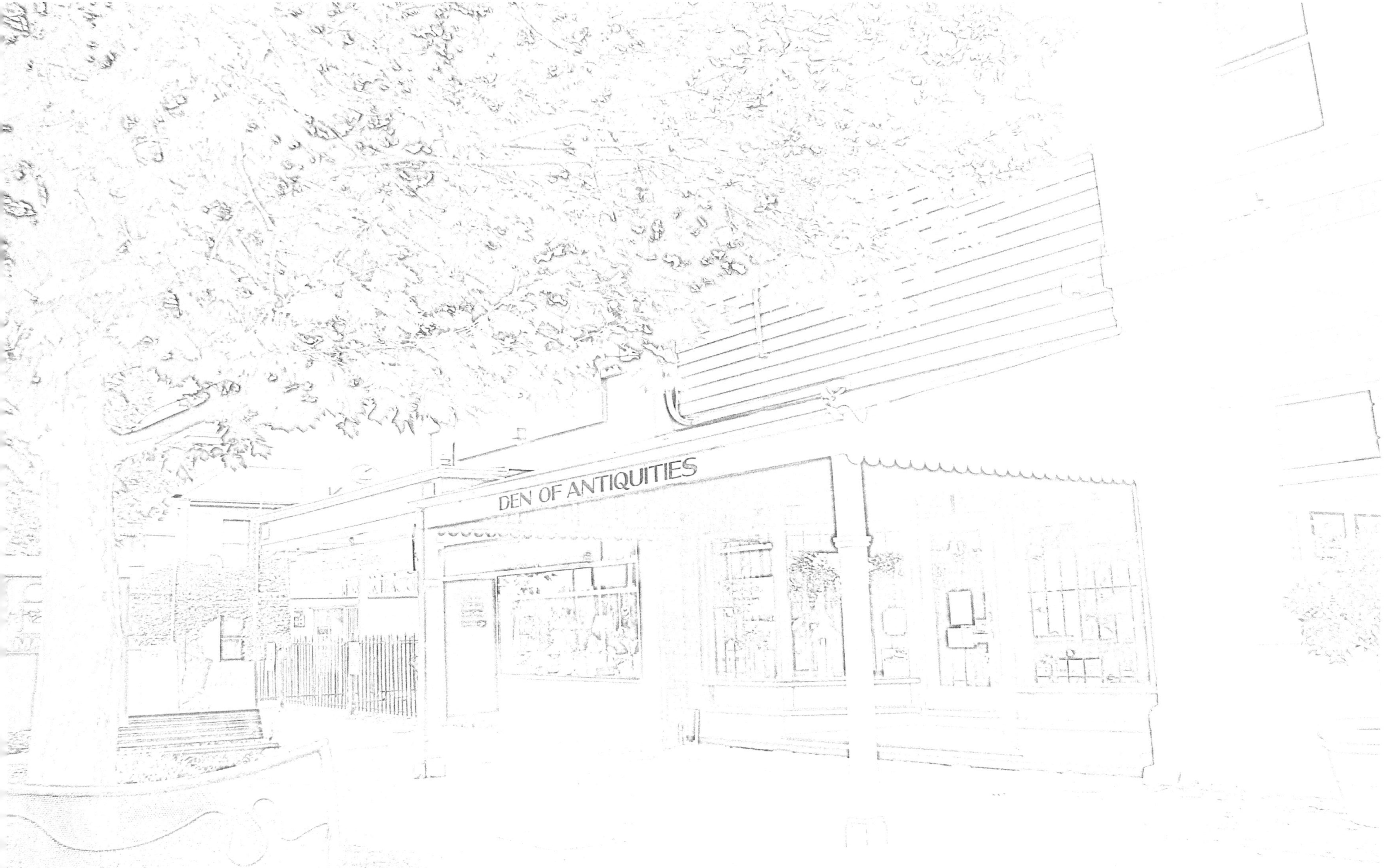
DEN OF ANTIQUITIES

CARLTON
Celebrated
PINEAPPLE BRAND
TREMBATH BROS.
GENERAL MERCHANTS
THE CORNER
STORES

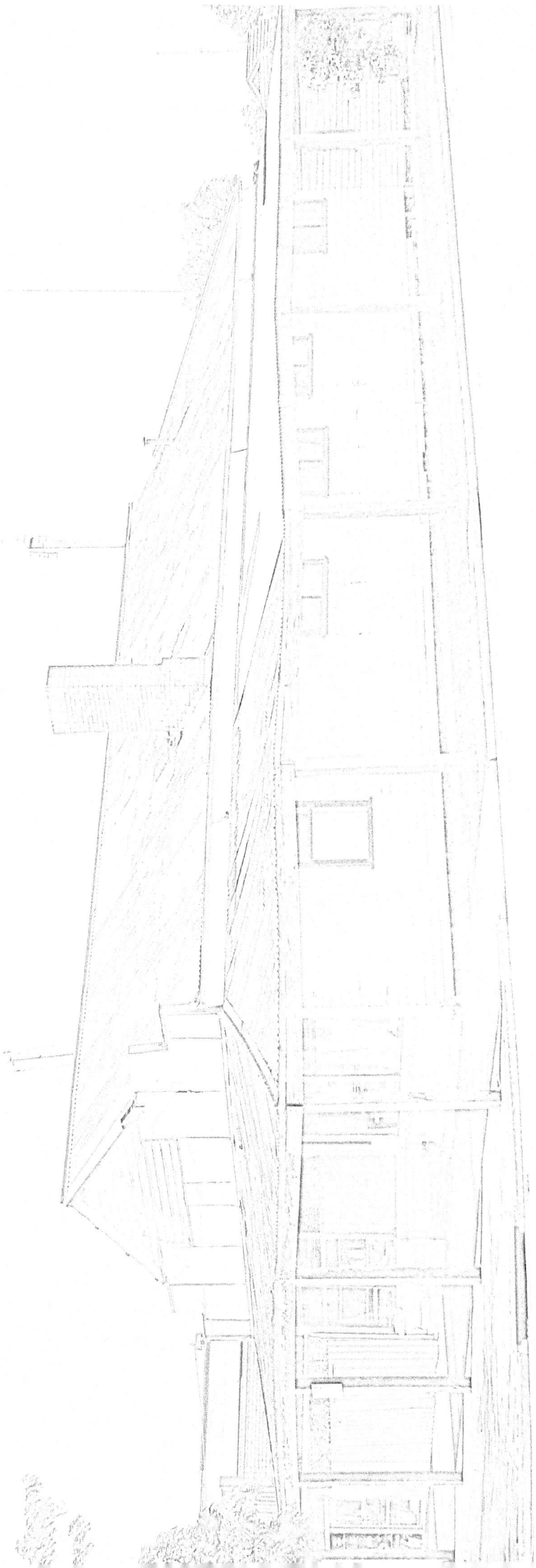

WARRACKNABEAL
POST OFFICE
POST
A GRATEFUL TRIBUTE
TO THE MEN OF THE
SHIRE OF BORUNG
WHO MADE THE
SUPREME SACRIFICE
IN THE
GREAT WAR

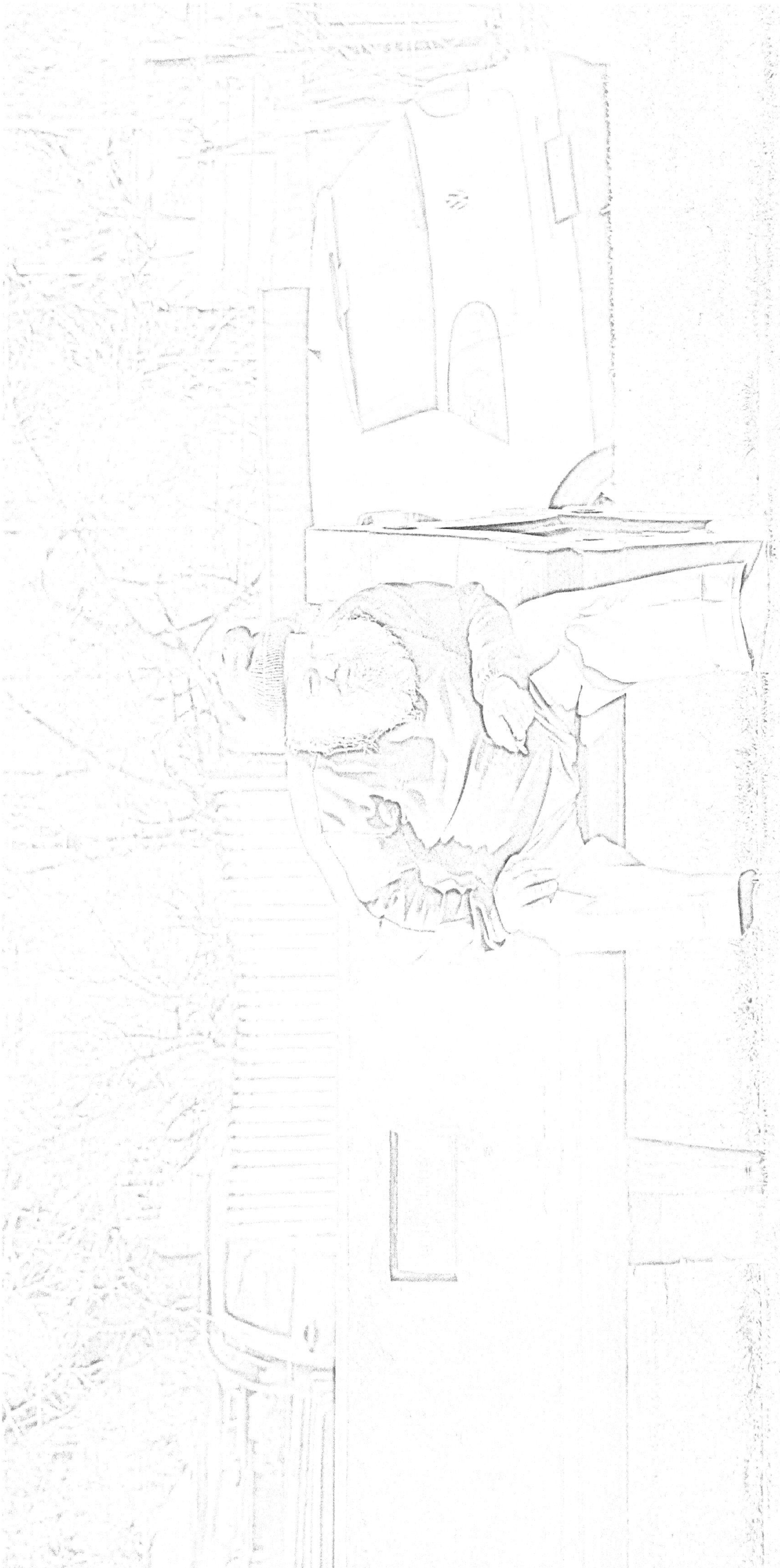

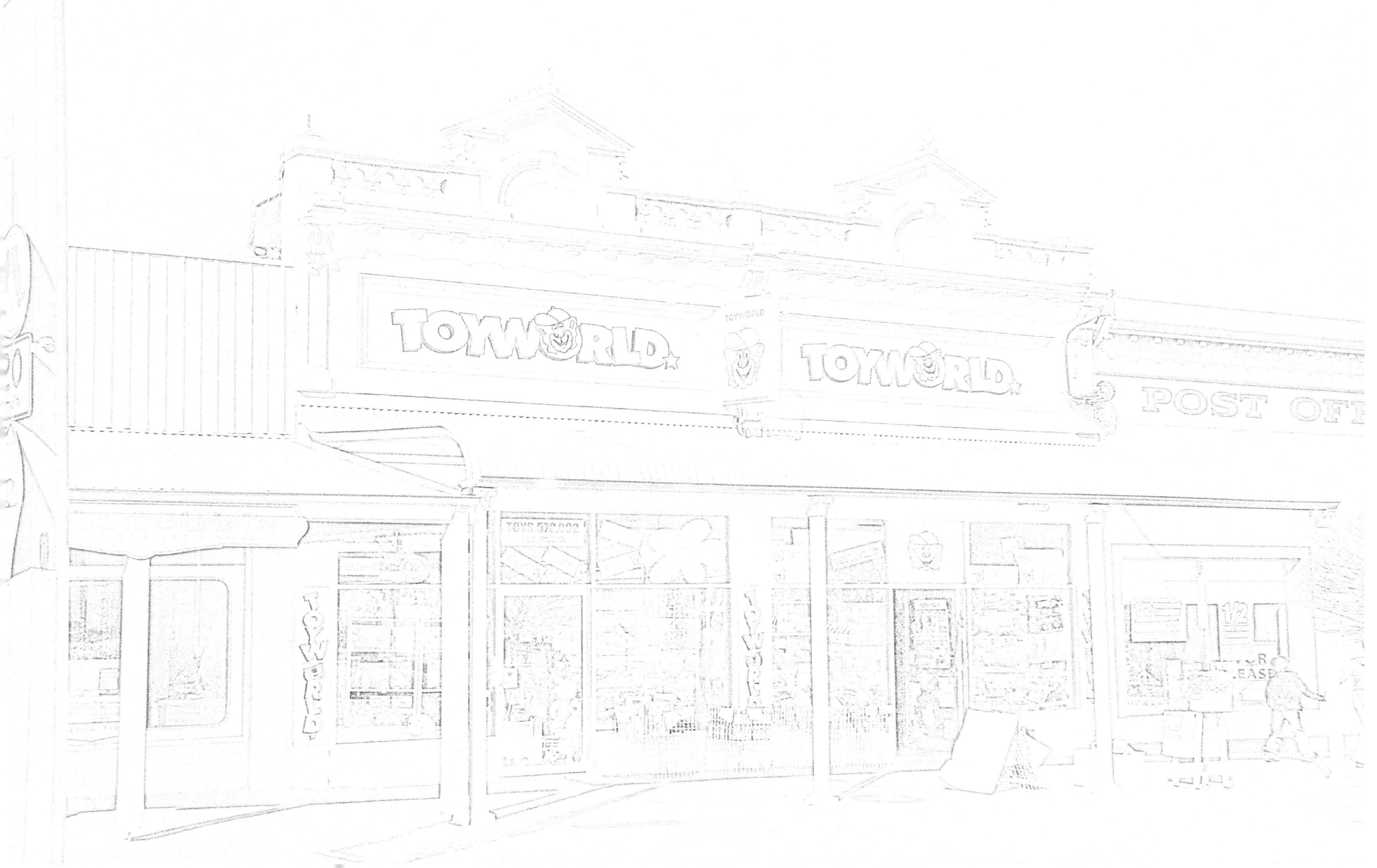
TOYWORLD
TOYWORLD
TOYWORLD
TOYWORLD
TOYWORLD

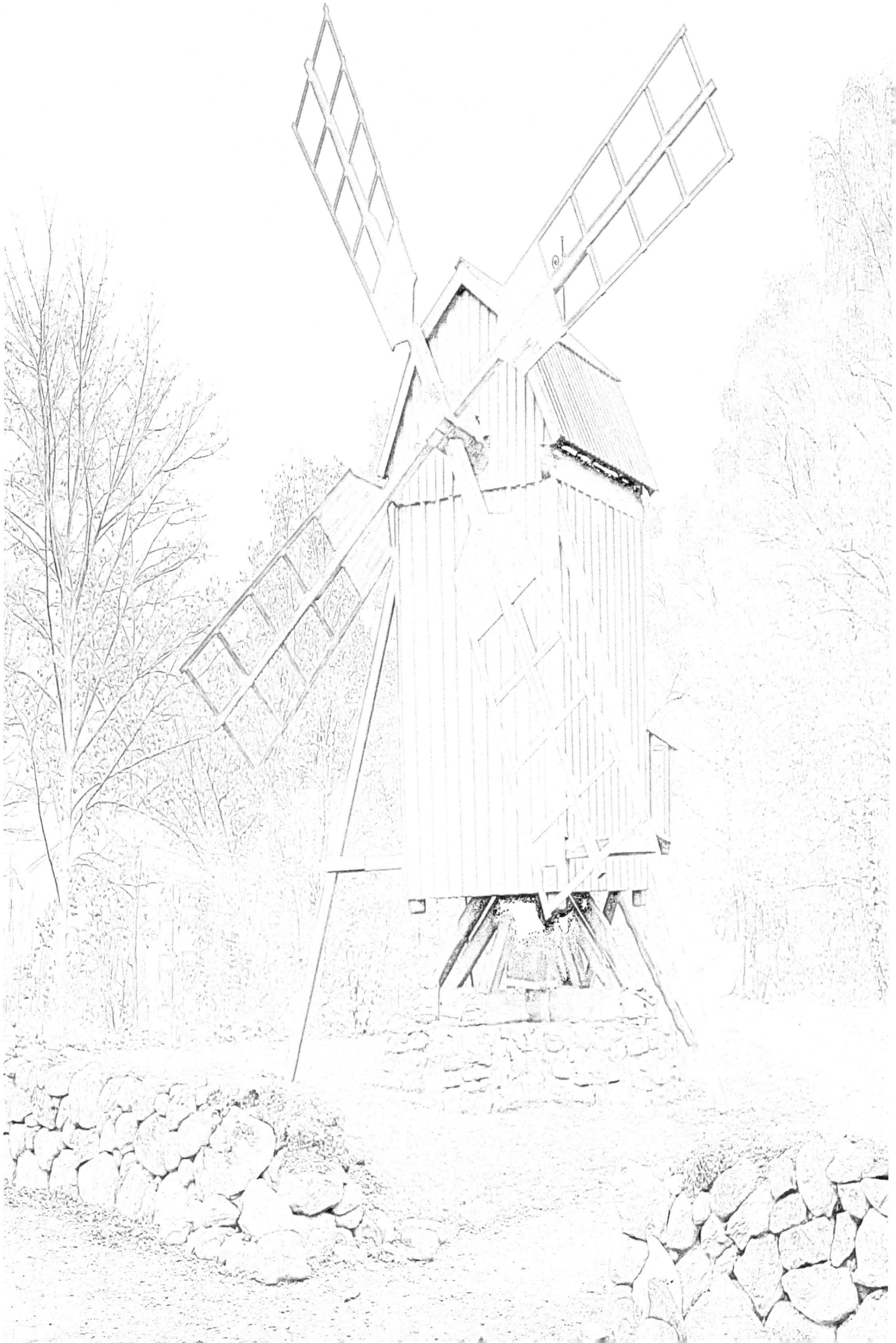

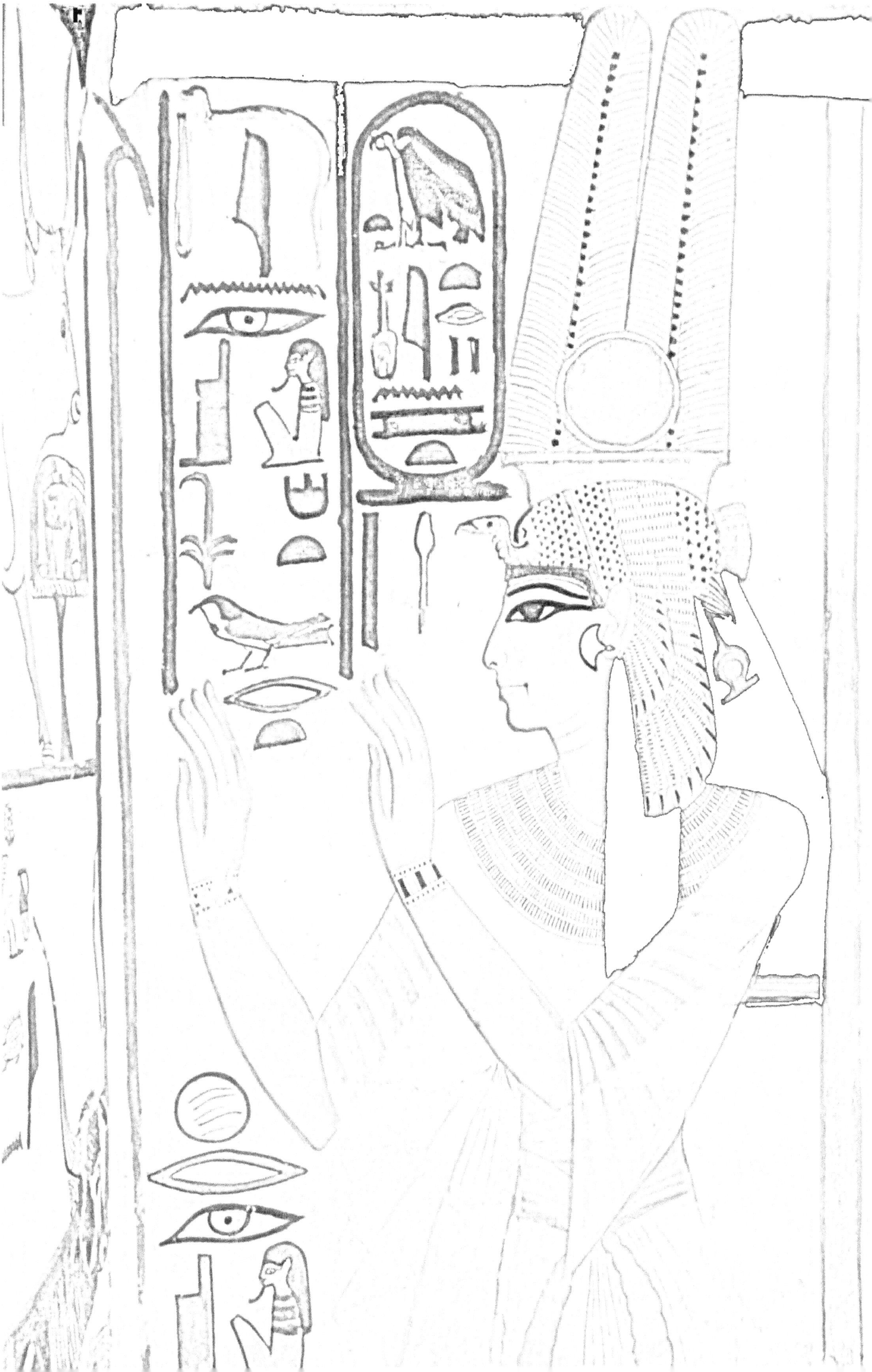

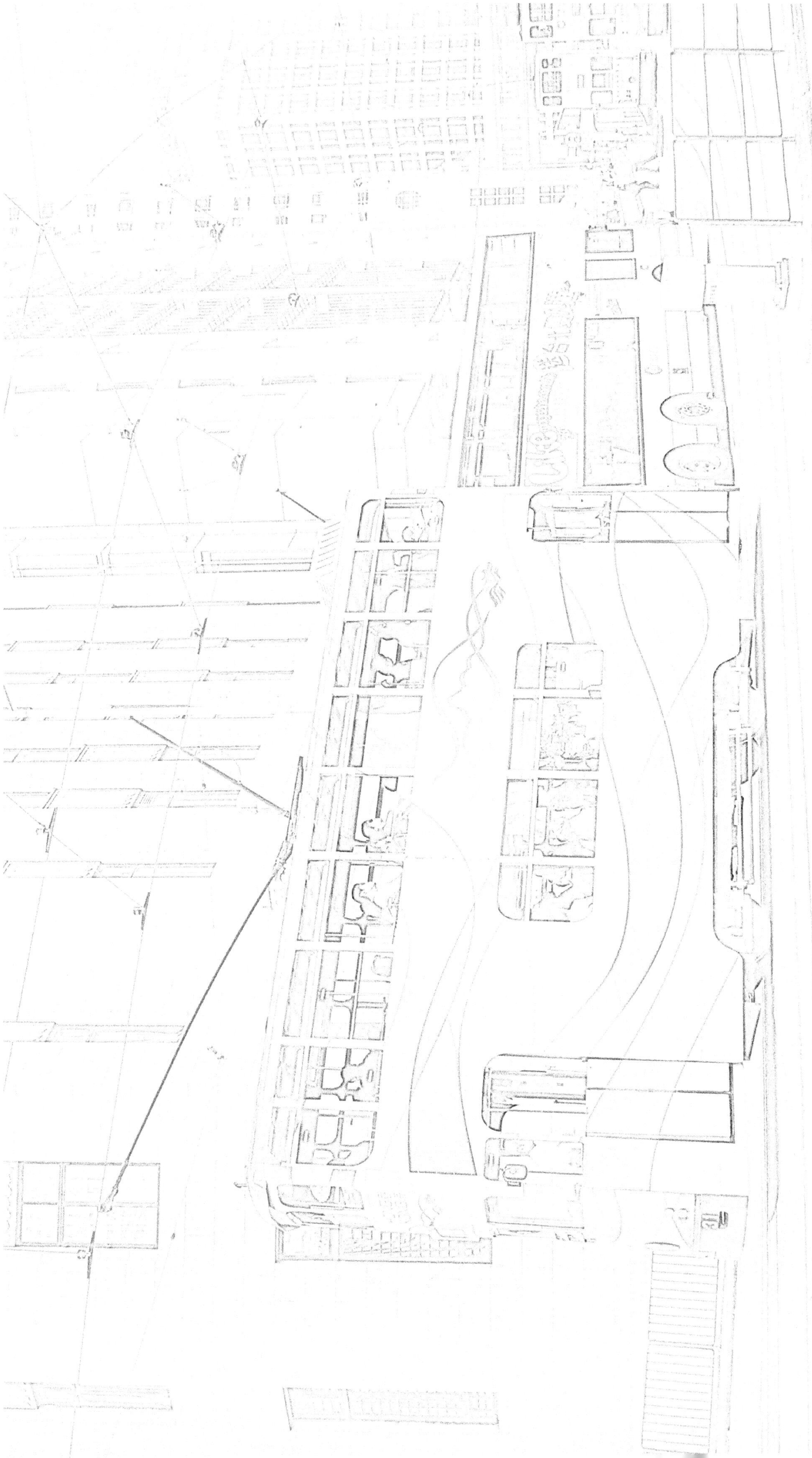

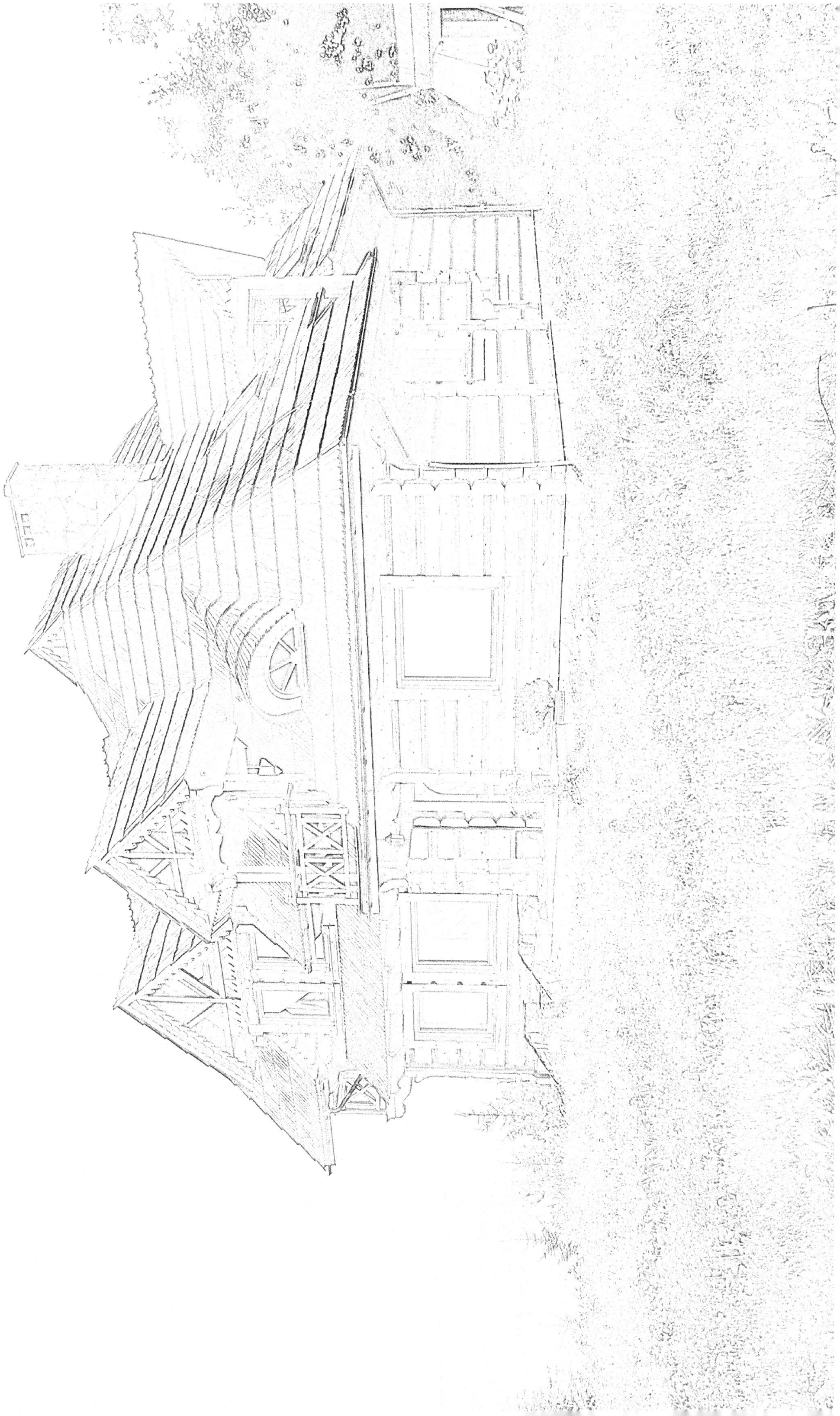

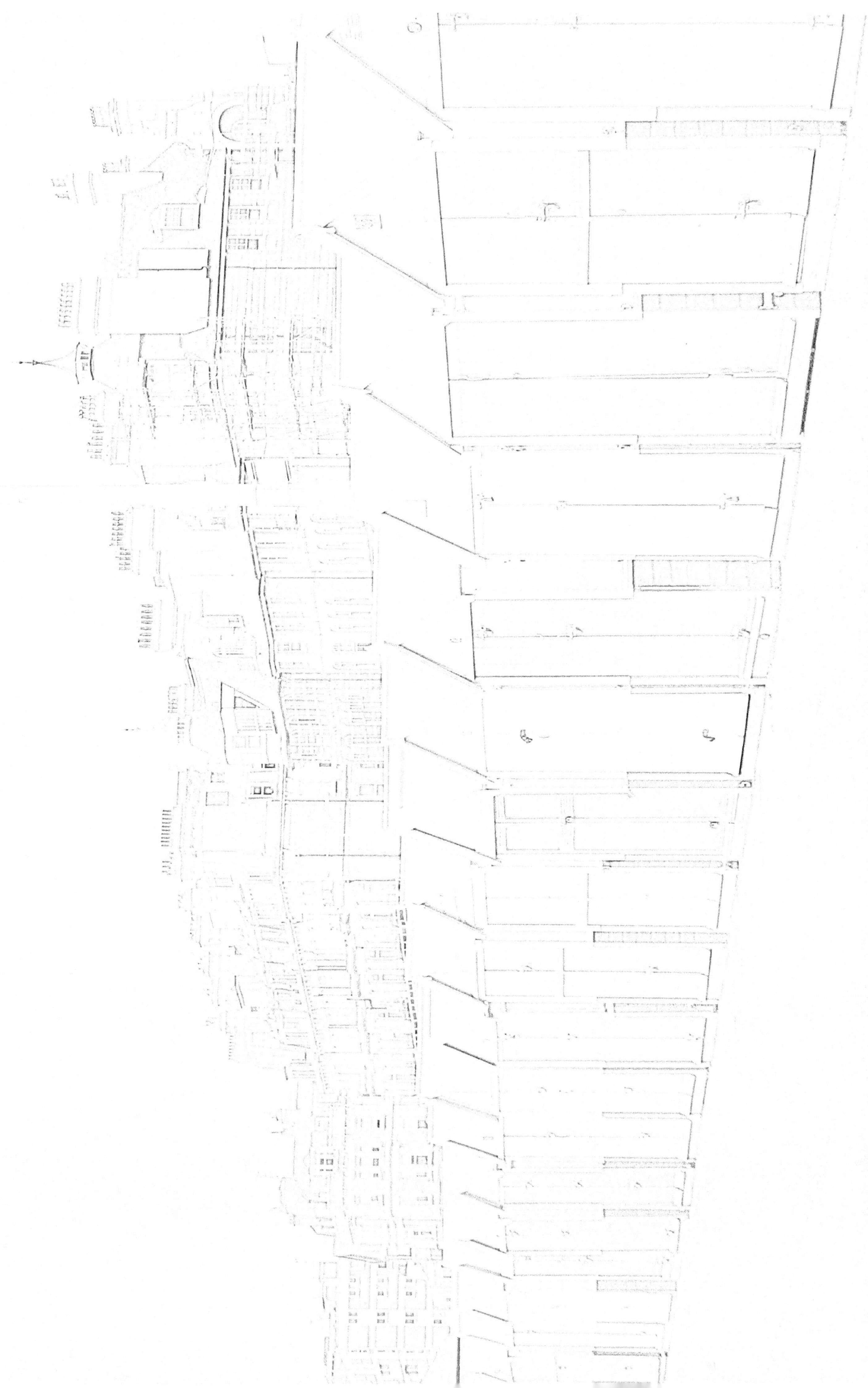

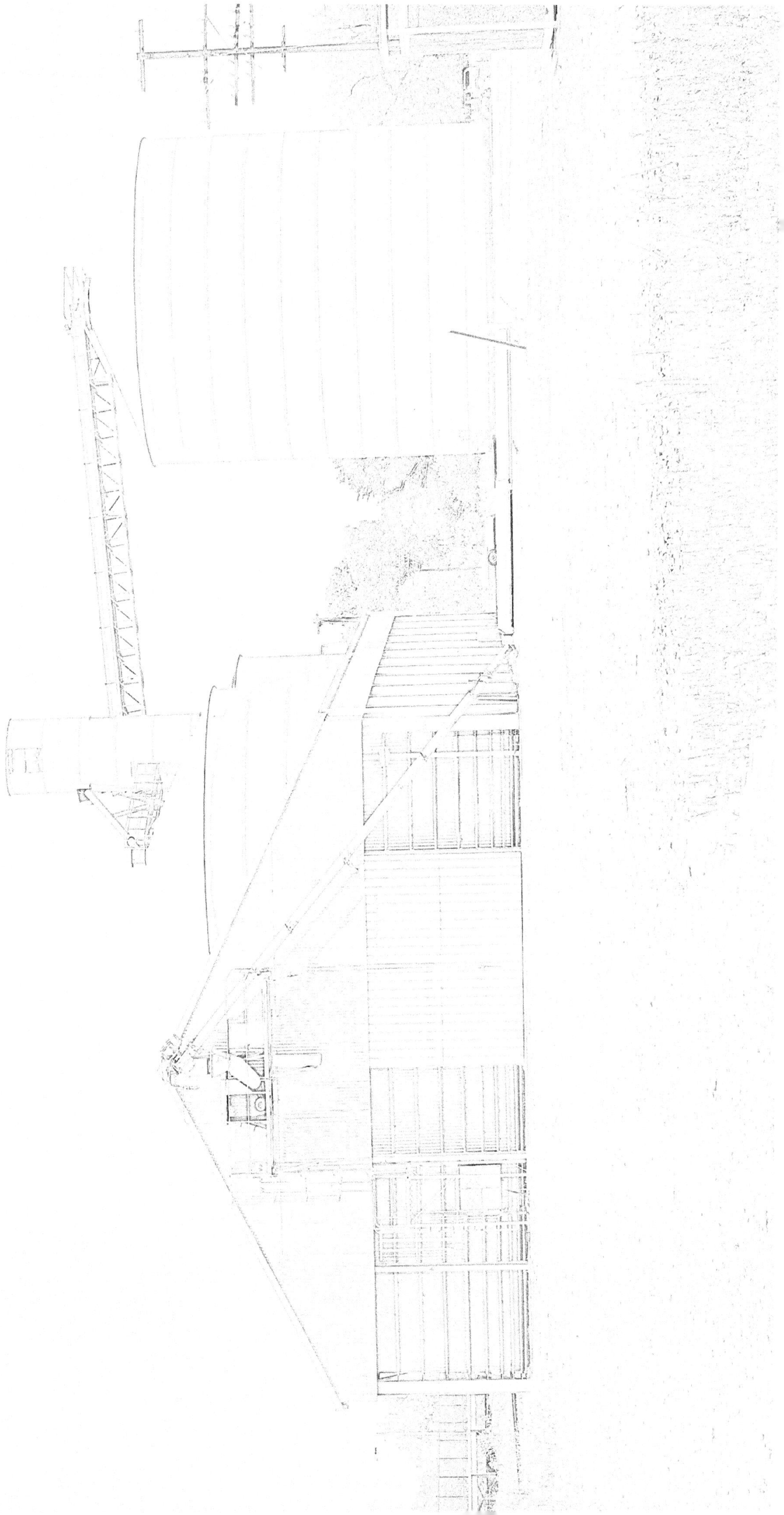

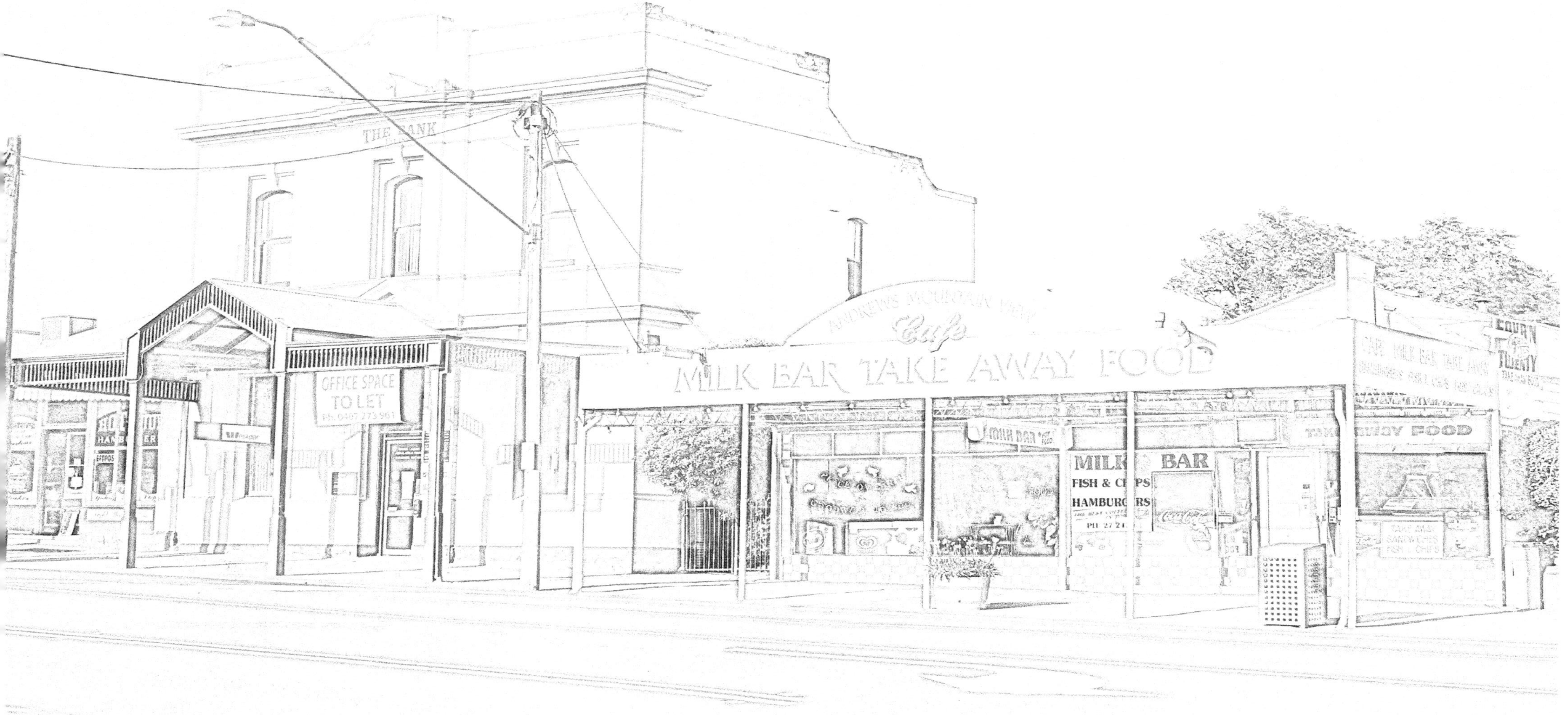
THE BANK
OFFICE SPACE
TO LET
Cafe
MILK BAR TAKE AWAY FOOD
MILK BAR
FISH & CHIPS
HAMBURGERS
MILK BAR
BAR

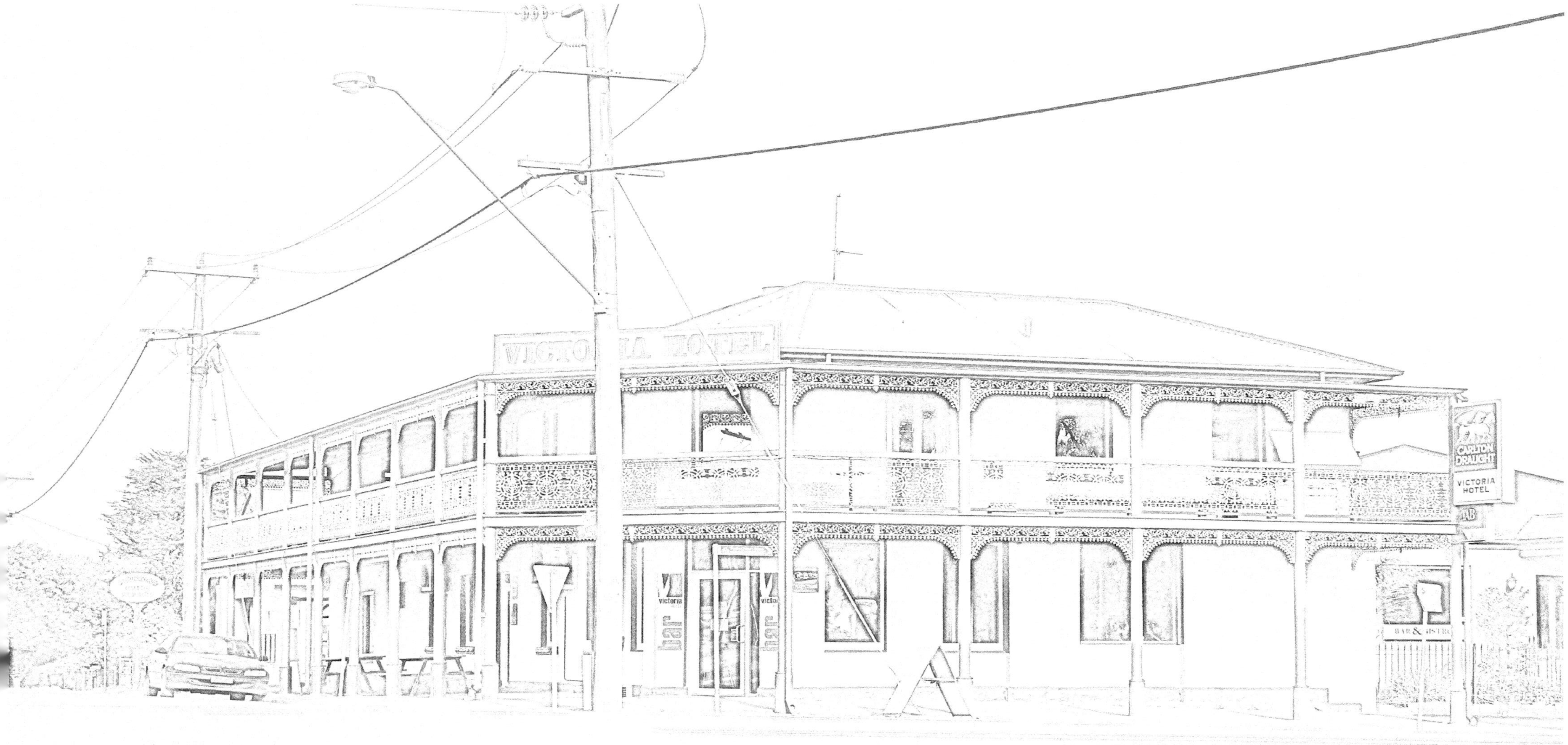
VICTORIA HOTEL
CARLTON DRAUGHT
VICTORIA HOTEL
victoria
bar
victoria
bar
BAR & BISTRO

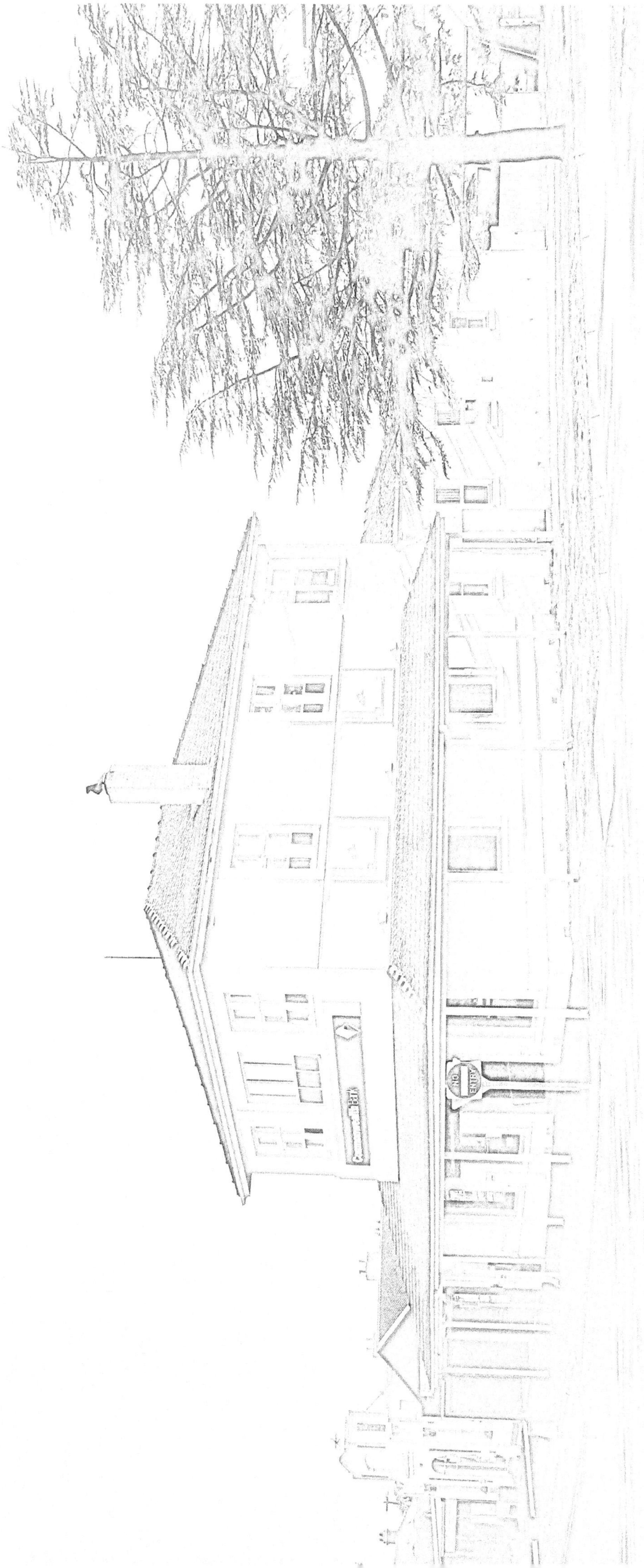

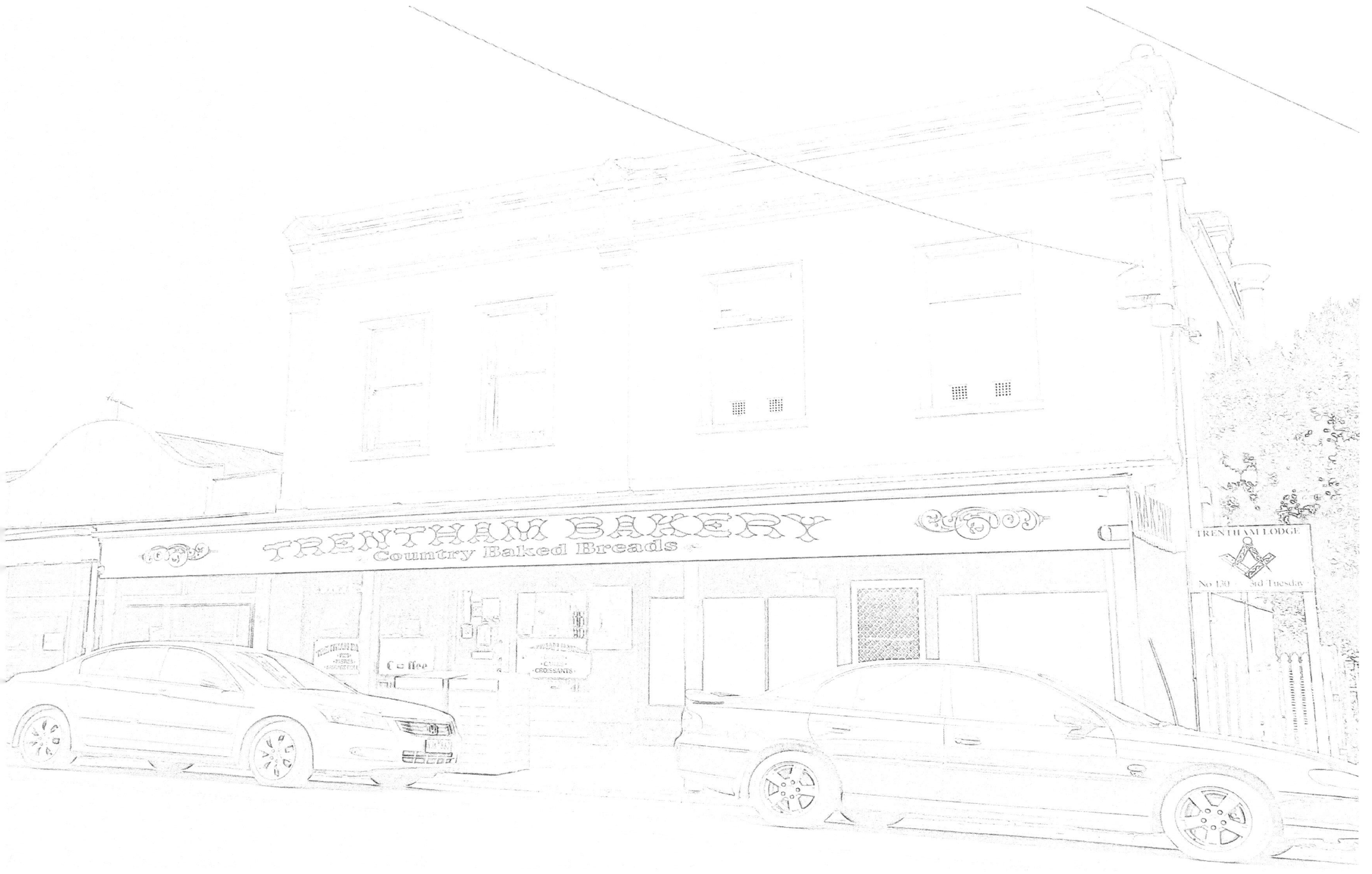
TRENTHAM BAKERY
Country Baked Breads
Coffee
CROSSANTS
TRENTHAM LODGE
No 130
3rd Tuesday

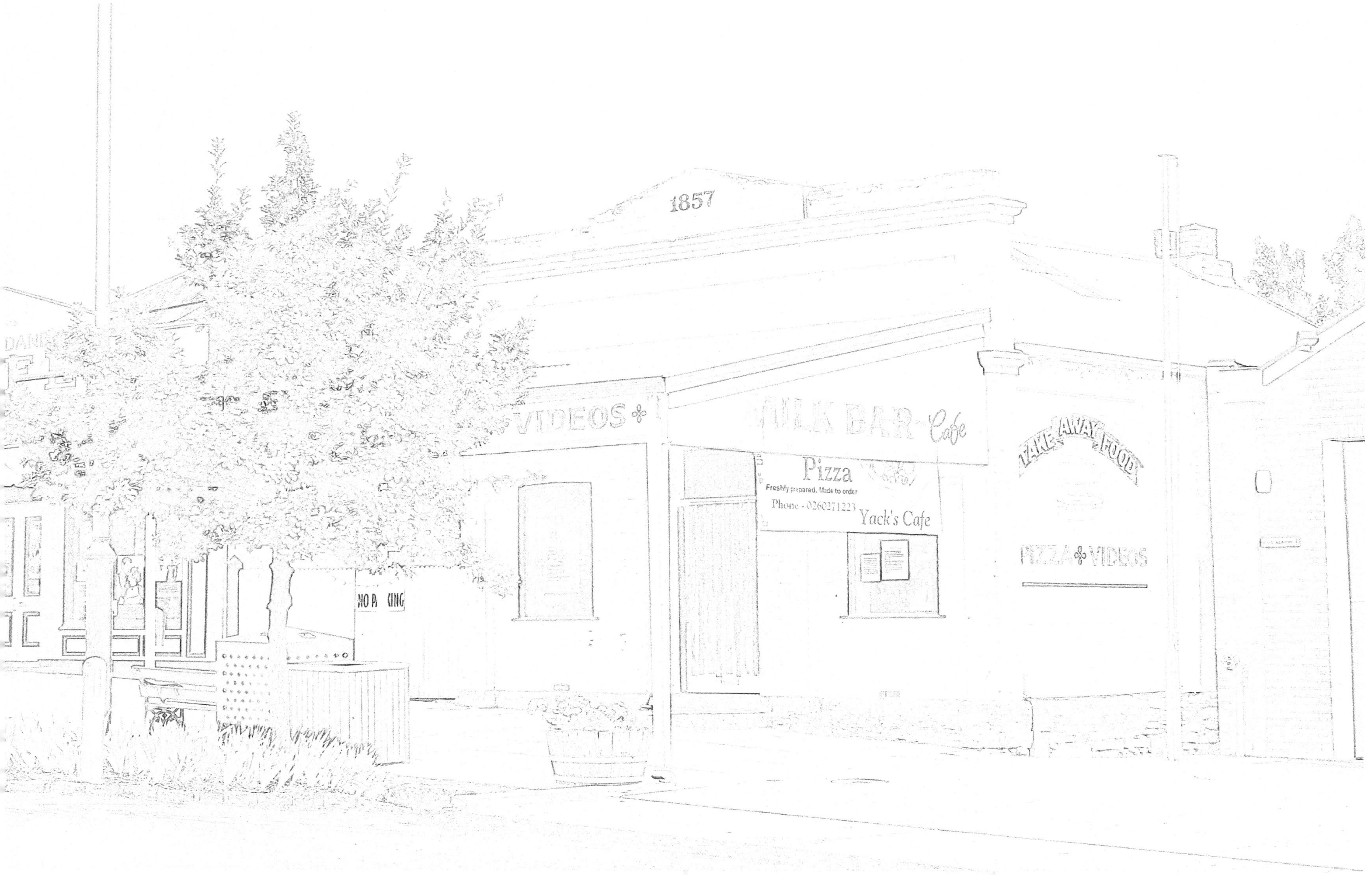
1857
VIDEOS
MILK BAR Cafe
Pizza
Freshly prepared, Made to order
Phone - 0260271223
Yack's Cafe
TAKE AWAY FOOD
PIZZA VIDEOS
NO PA KING

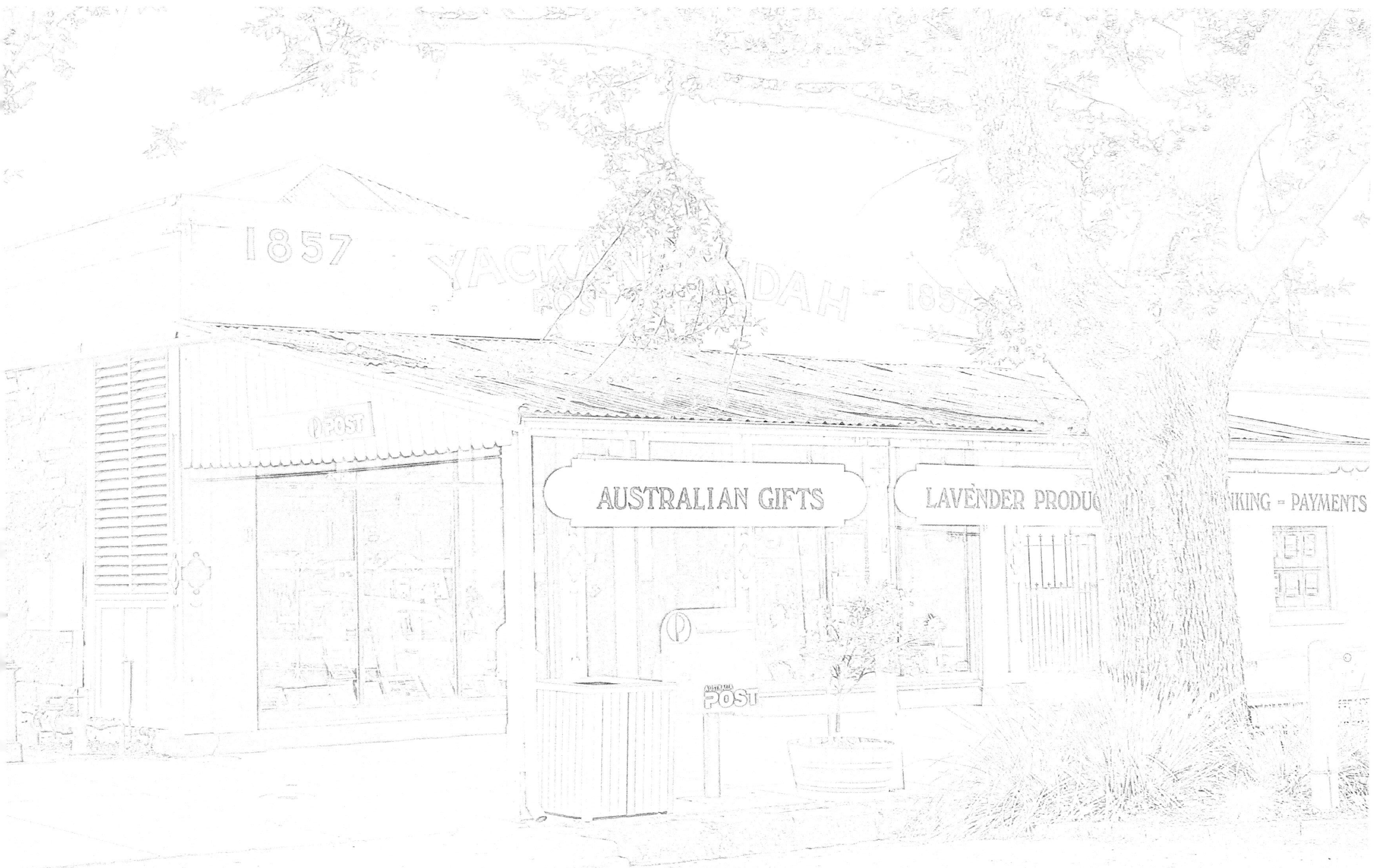
1857
POST
AUSTRALIAN GIFTS
LAVENDER PRODUC
NKING - PAYMENTS
POST

25

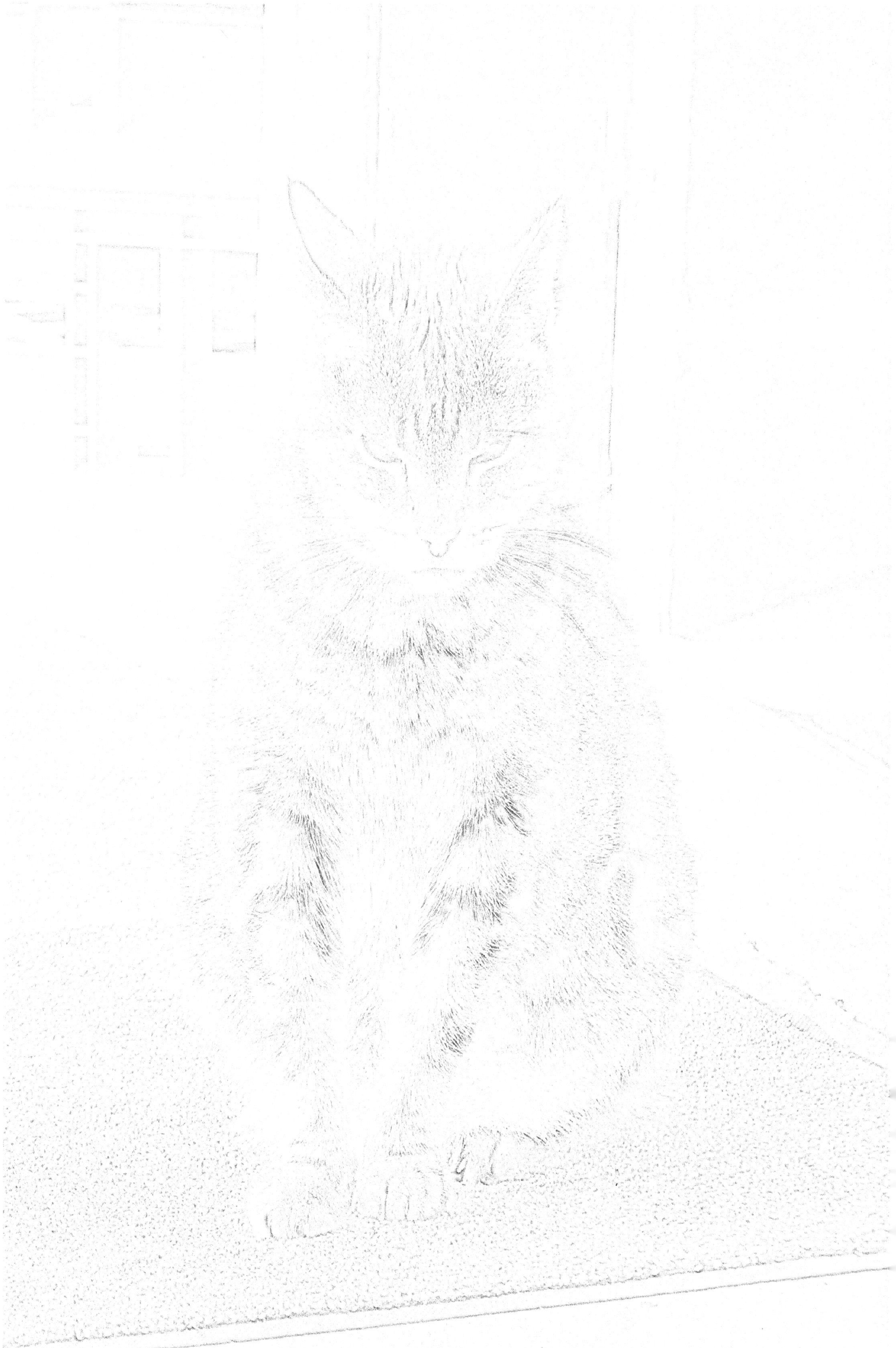

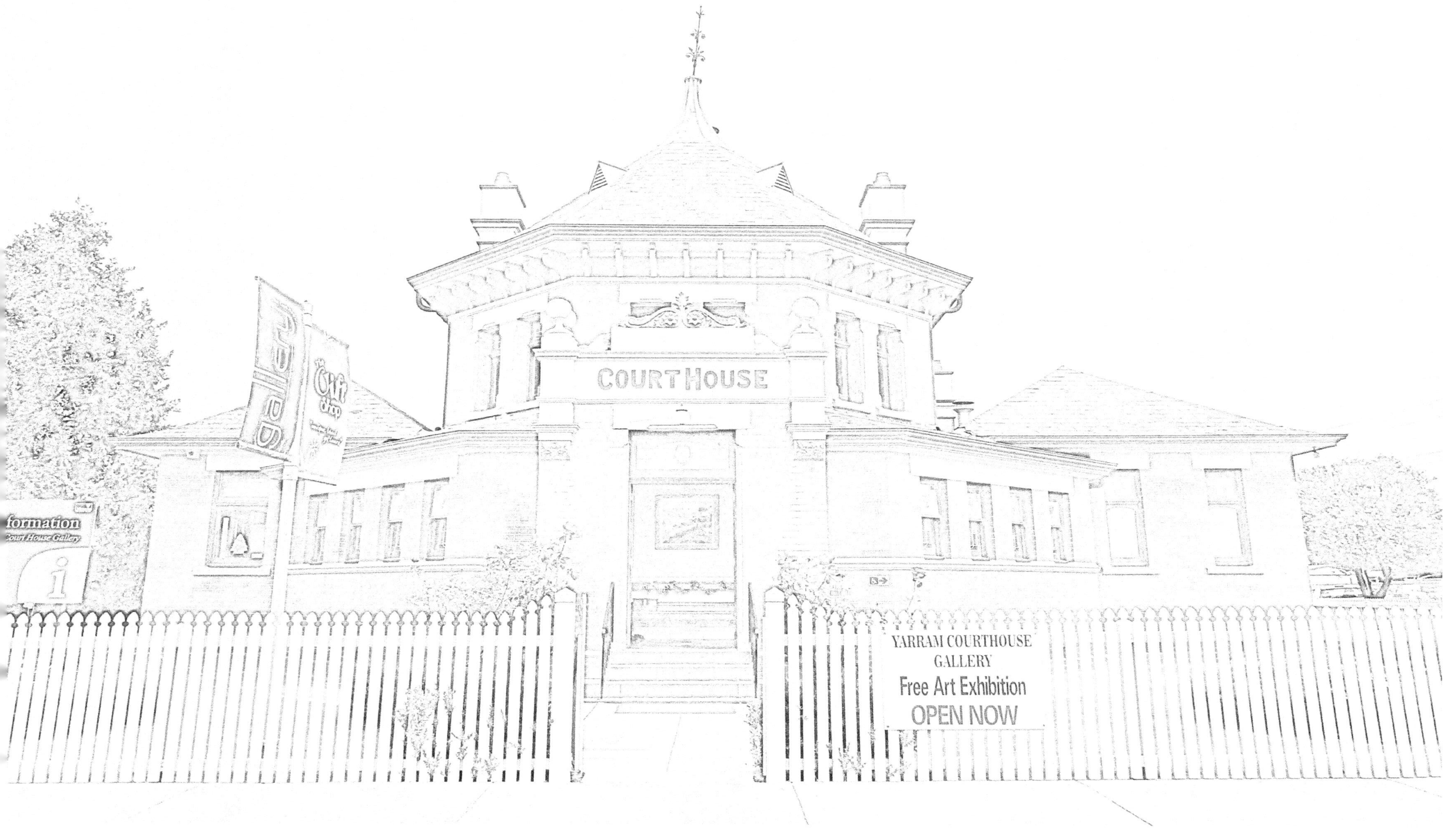
COURT HOUSE
formation
Court House Gallery
i
Gift Shop
YARRAM COURTHOUSE
GALLERY
Free Art Exhibition
OPEN NOW

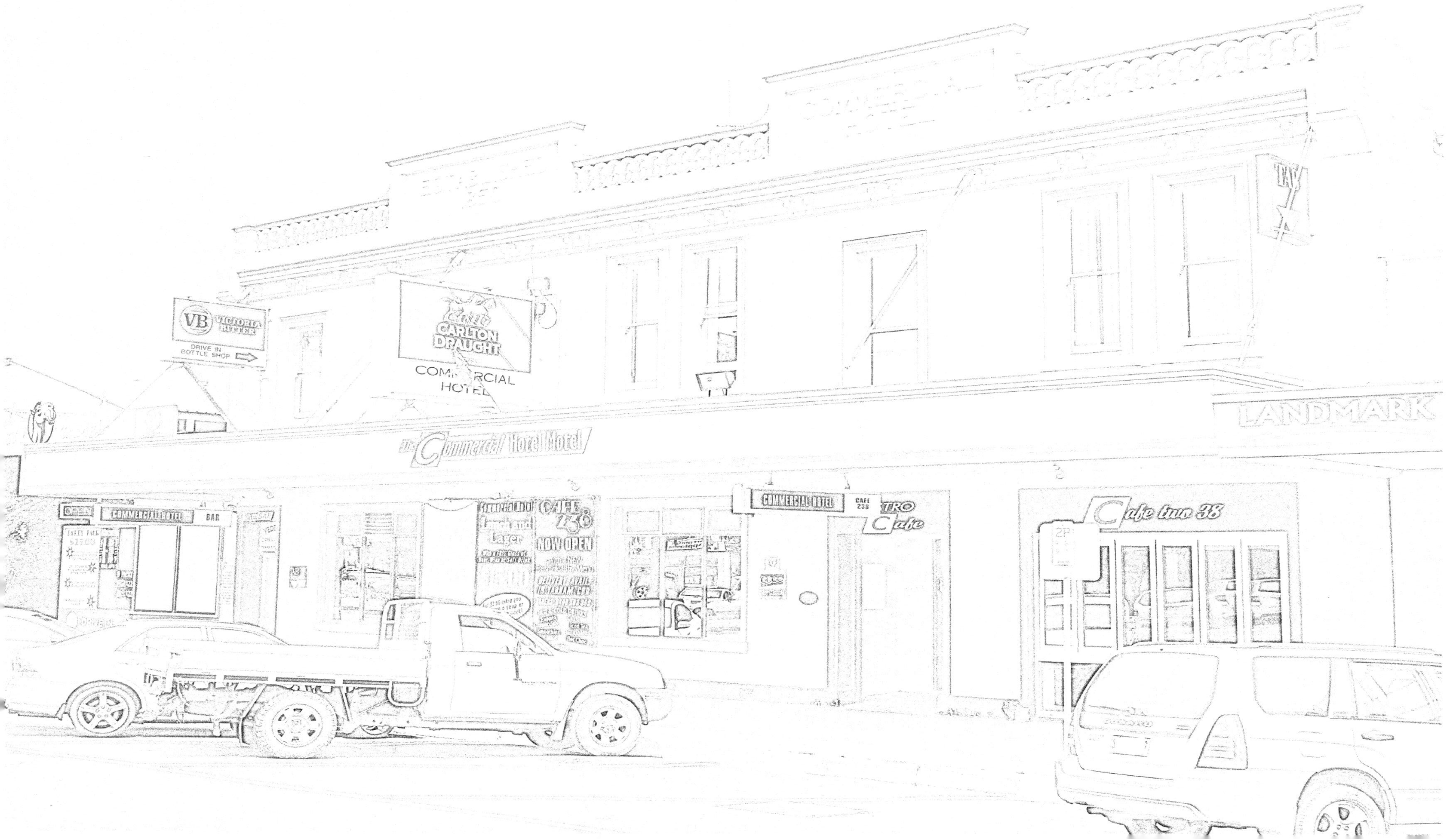
VB VICTORIA BITTER
DRIVE IN BOTTLE SHOP
CARLTON DRAUGHT
COMMERCIAL HOTEL
The Commercial Hotel Motel
LANDMARK
COMMERCIAL HOTEL
BAR
CAFE 238
NOW OPEN
COMMERCIAL HOTEL
CAFE 238
TRO Cafe
Cafe two 38
2P

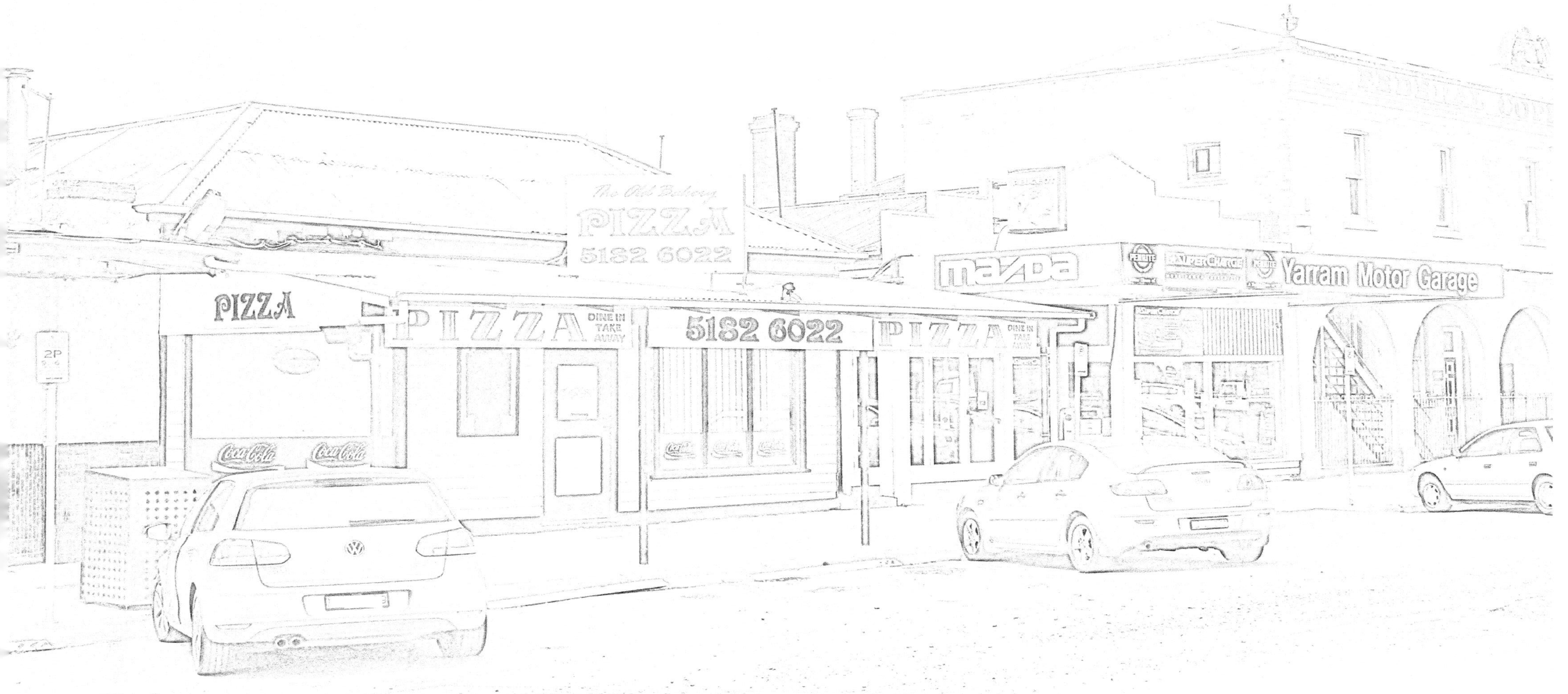
The Old Bakery
PIZZA
5182 6022
PIZZA
PIZZA
DINE IN
TAKE AWAY
5182 6022
PIZZA
Coca-Cola
Coca-Cola
2P
mazda
Yarram Motor Garage

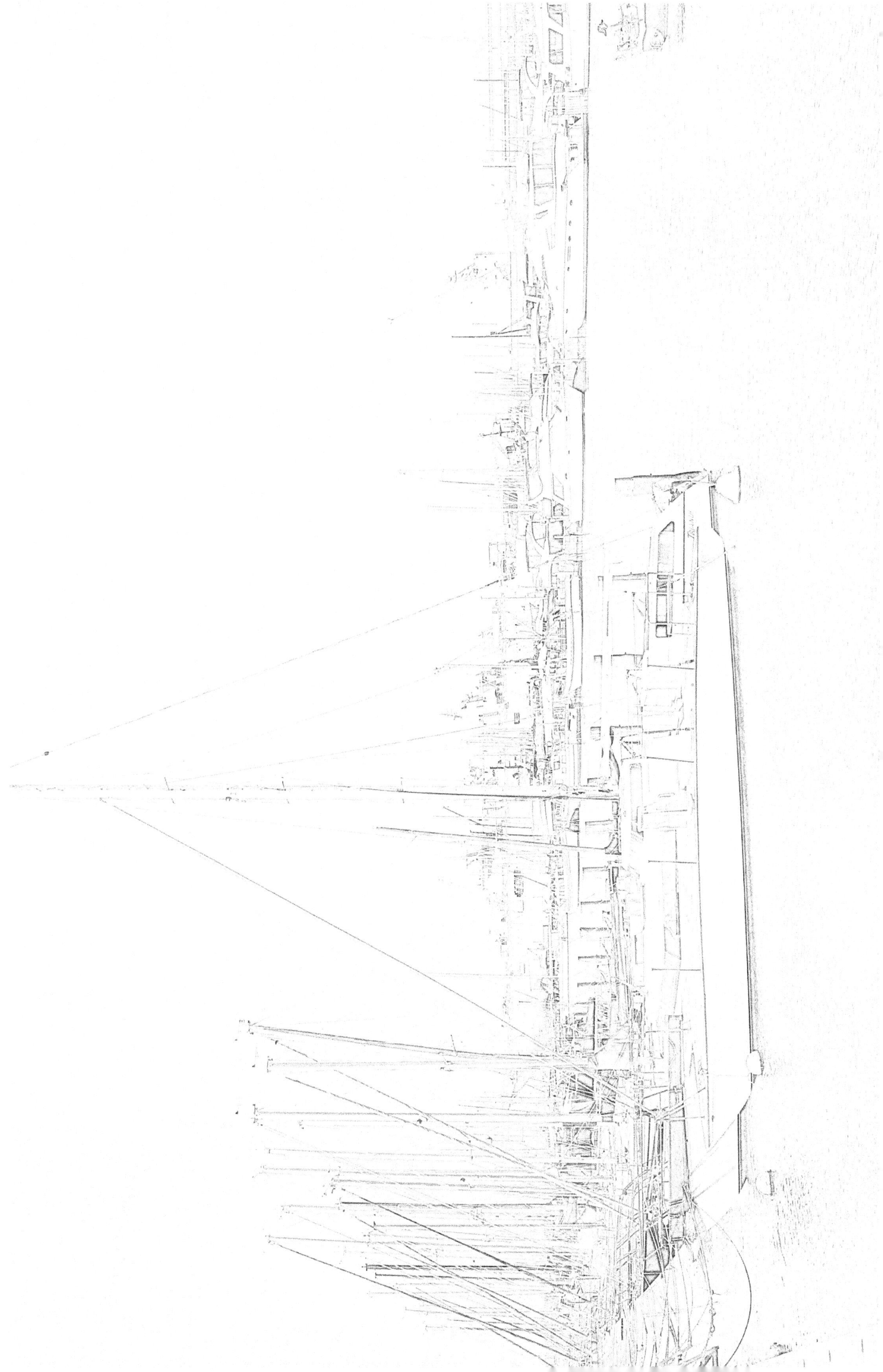

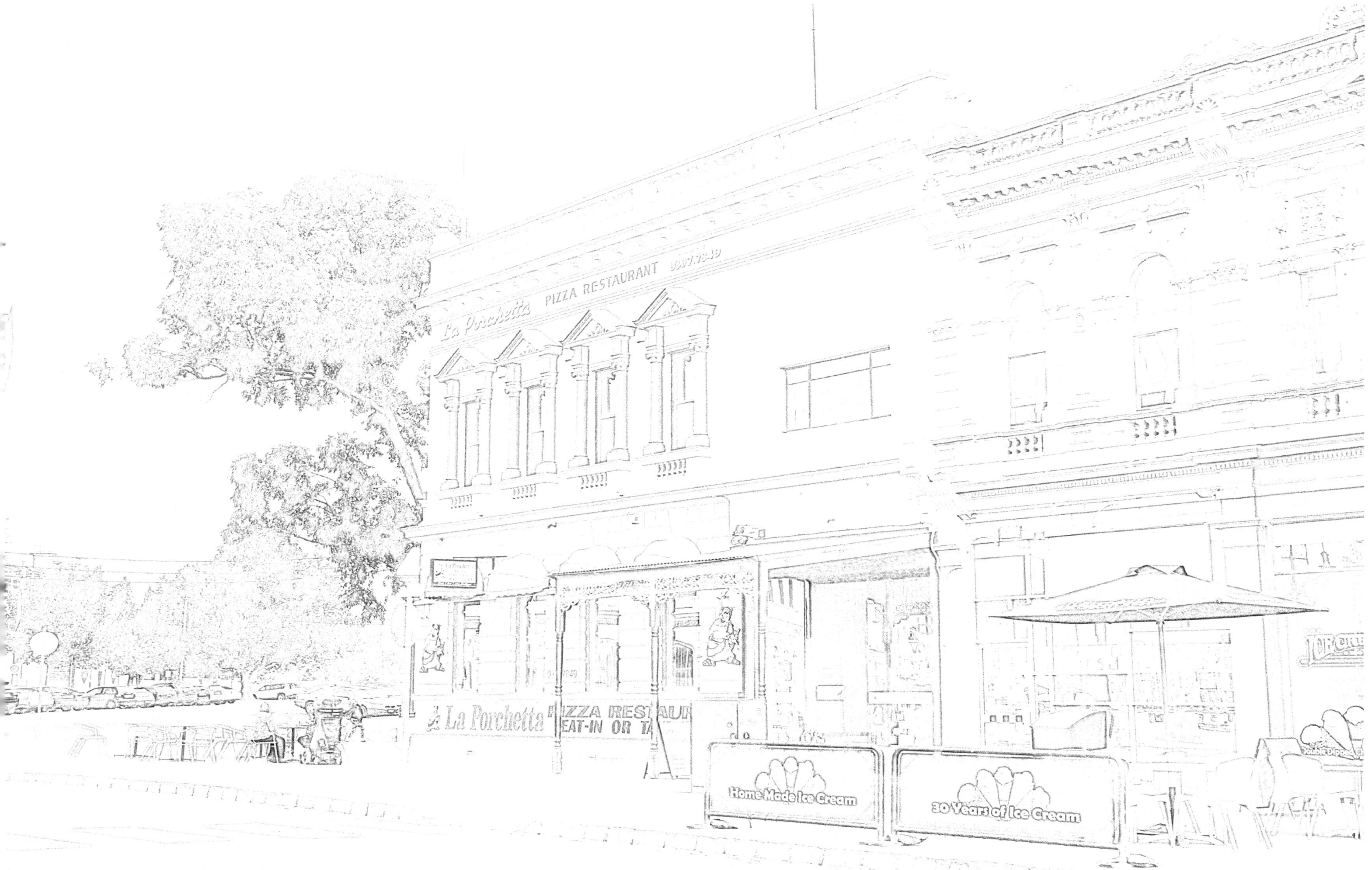
La Porchetta PIZZA RESTAURANT
La Porchetta PIZZA RESTAUR
EAT-IN OR TA
Home Made Ice Cream
30 Years of Ice Cream

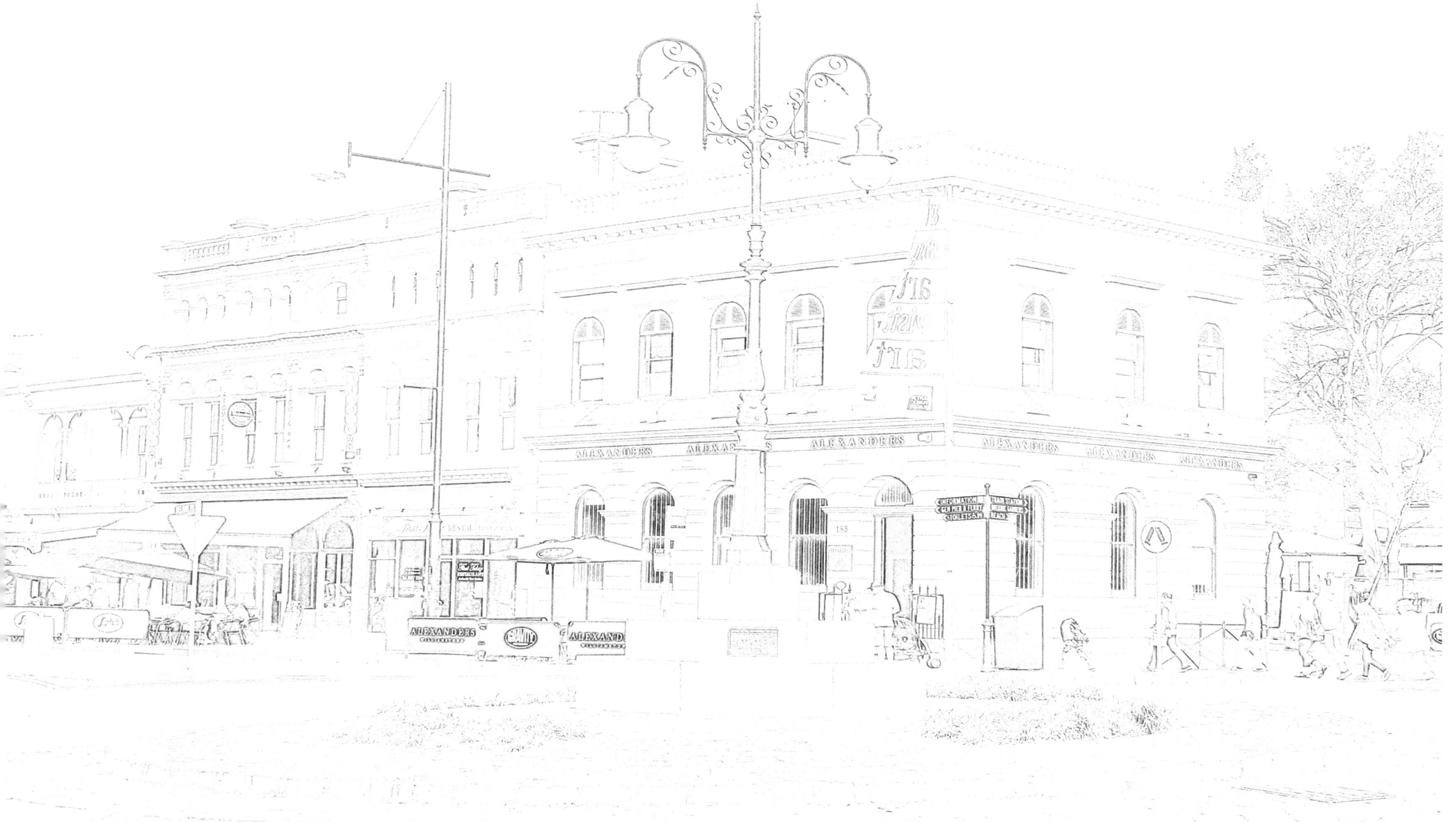

ALEXANDERS
ALEXANDERS
ALEXANDERS
ALEXANDERS
ALEXANDERS
ALEXANDERS
INFORMATION
GEM PIER & FERRY
TOILETS
TRAIN STATION
BEACH
189
ALEXANDERS
GRAVITY

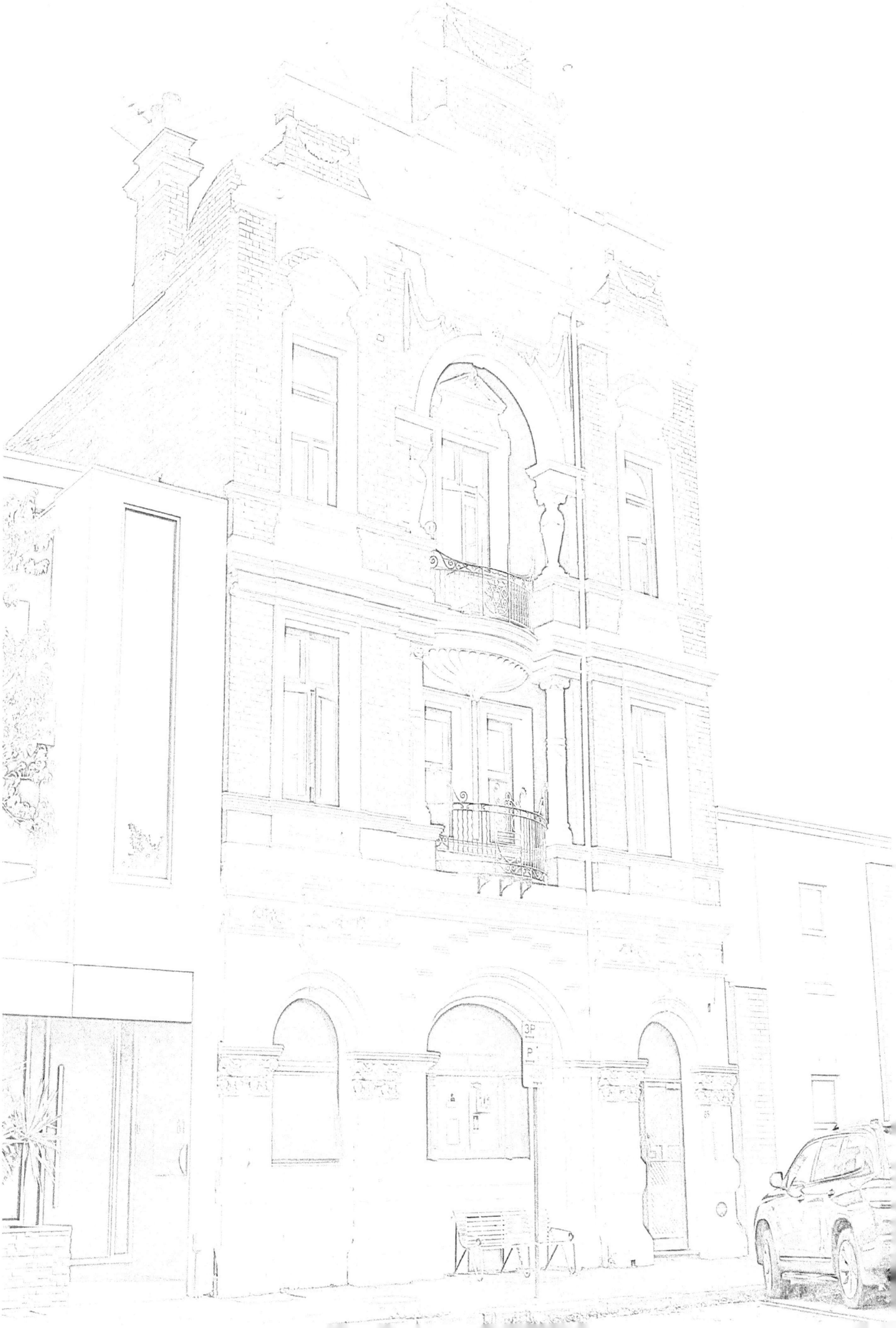
3P
P

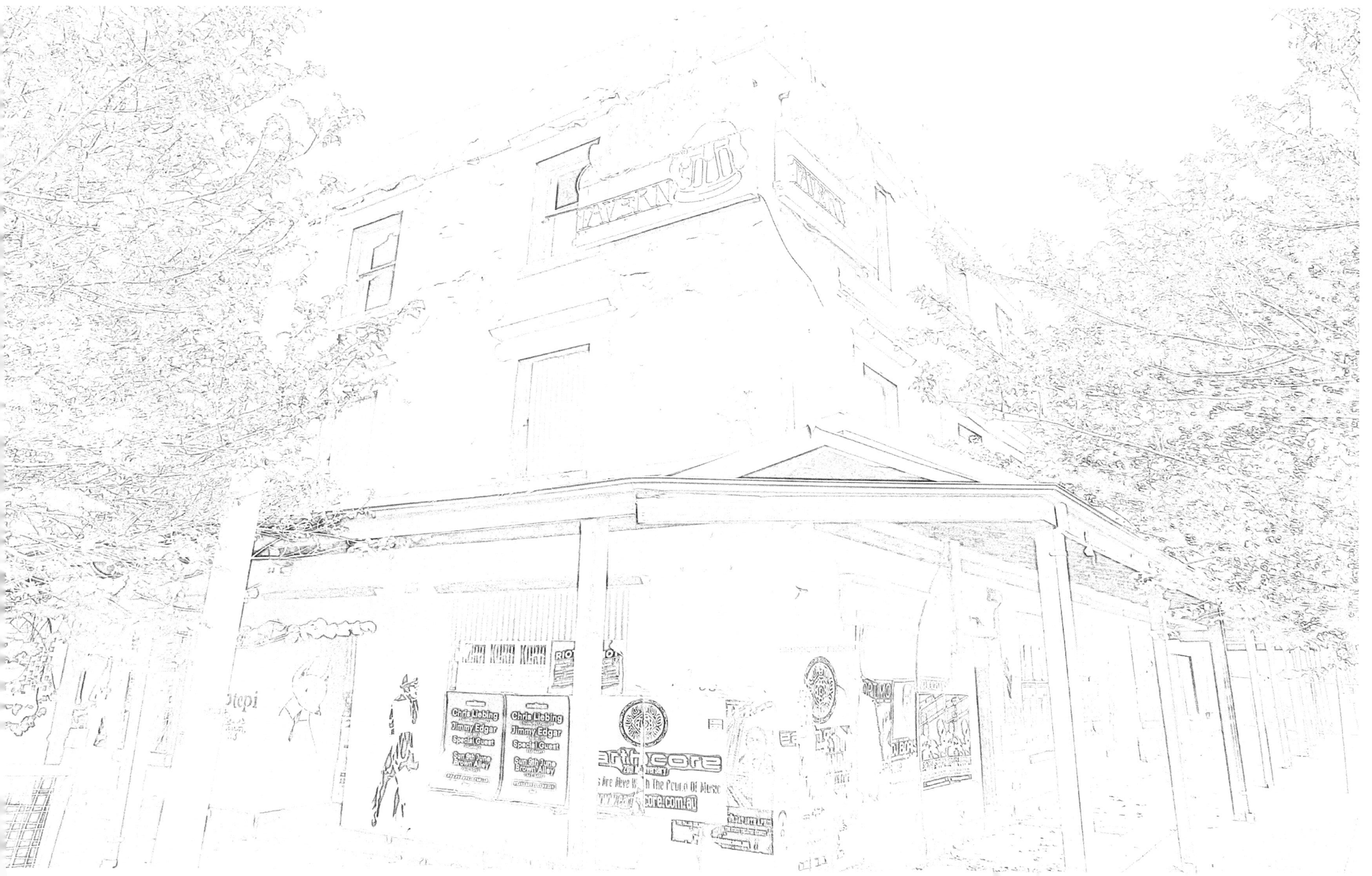
TAVERN
Chris Liebing
Jimmy Edgar
Special Guest
Sun 9th June
Brown Alley
Chris Liebing
Jimmy Edgar
Special Guest
Sun 9th June
Brown Alley

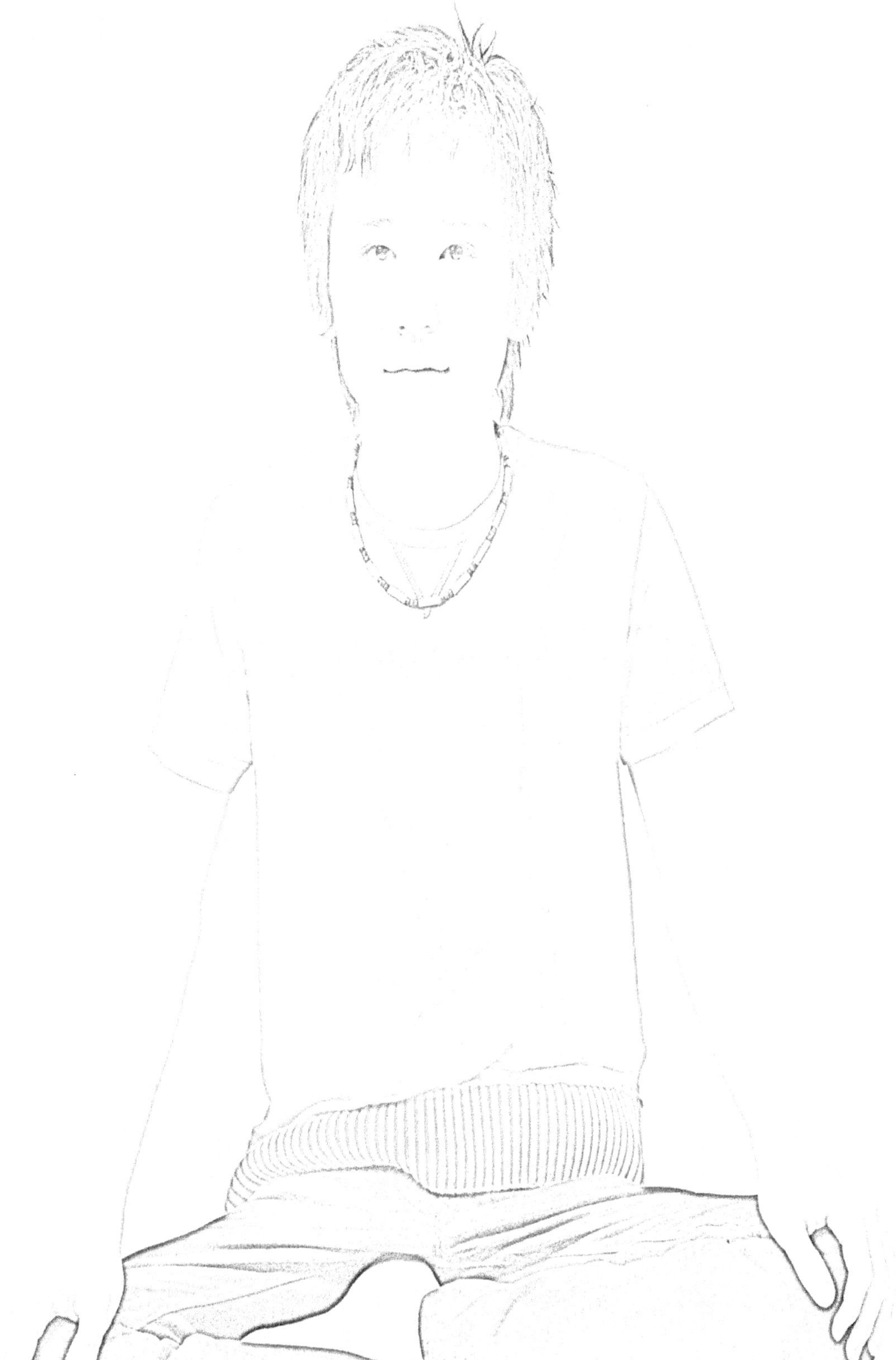

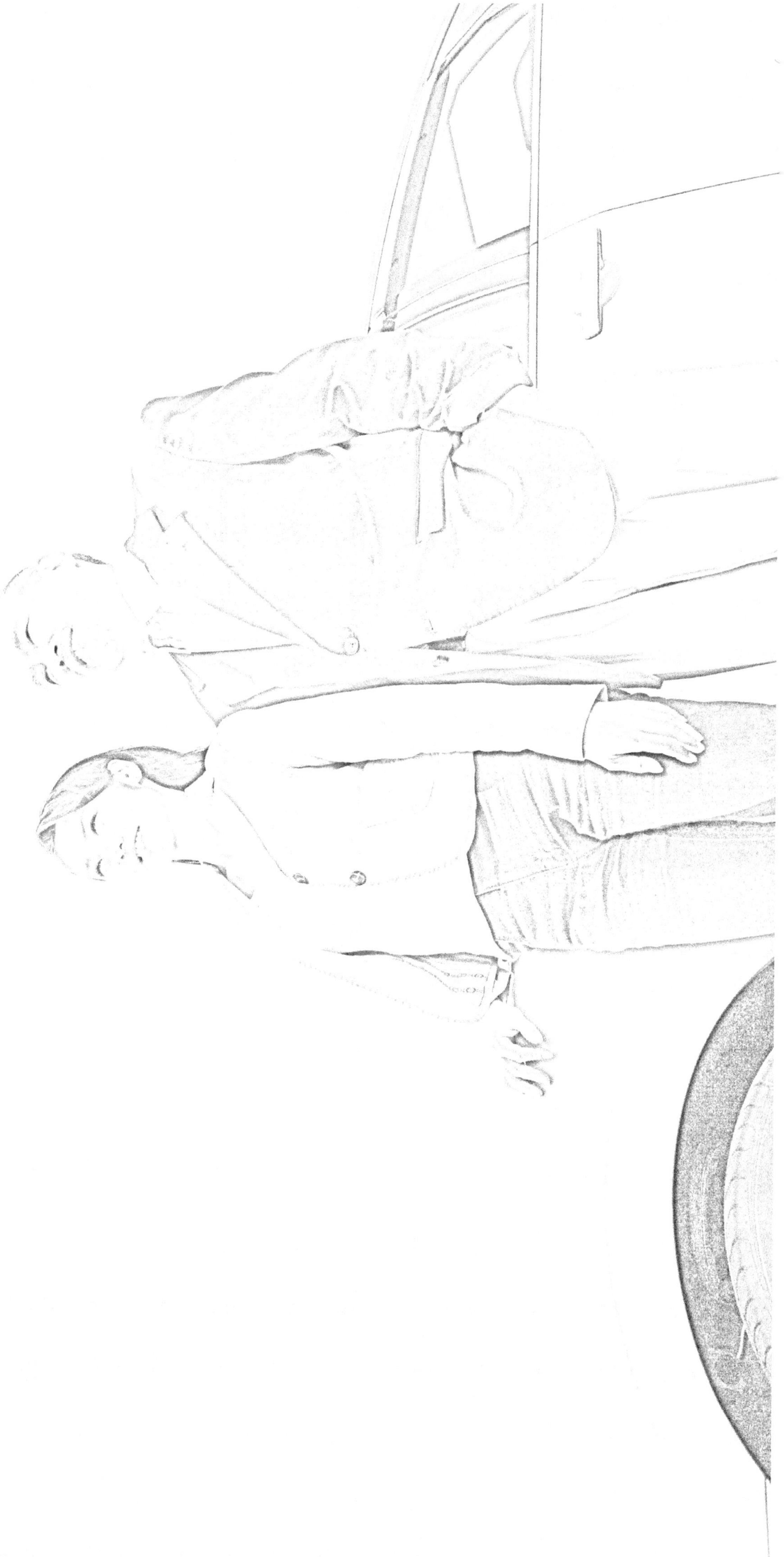

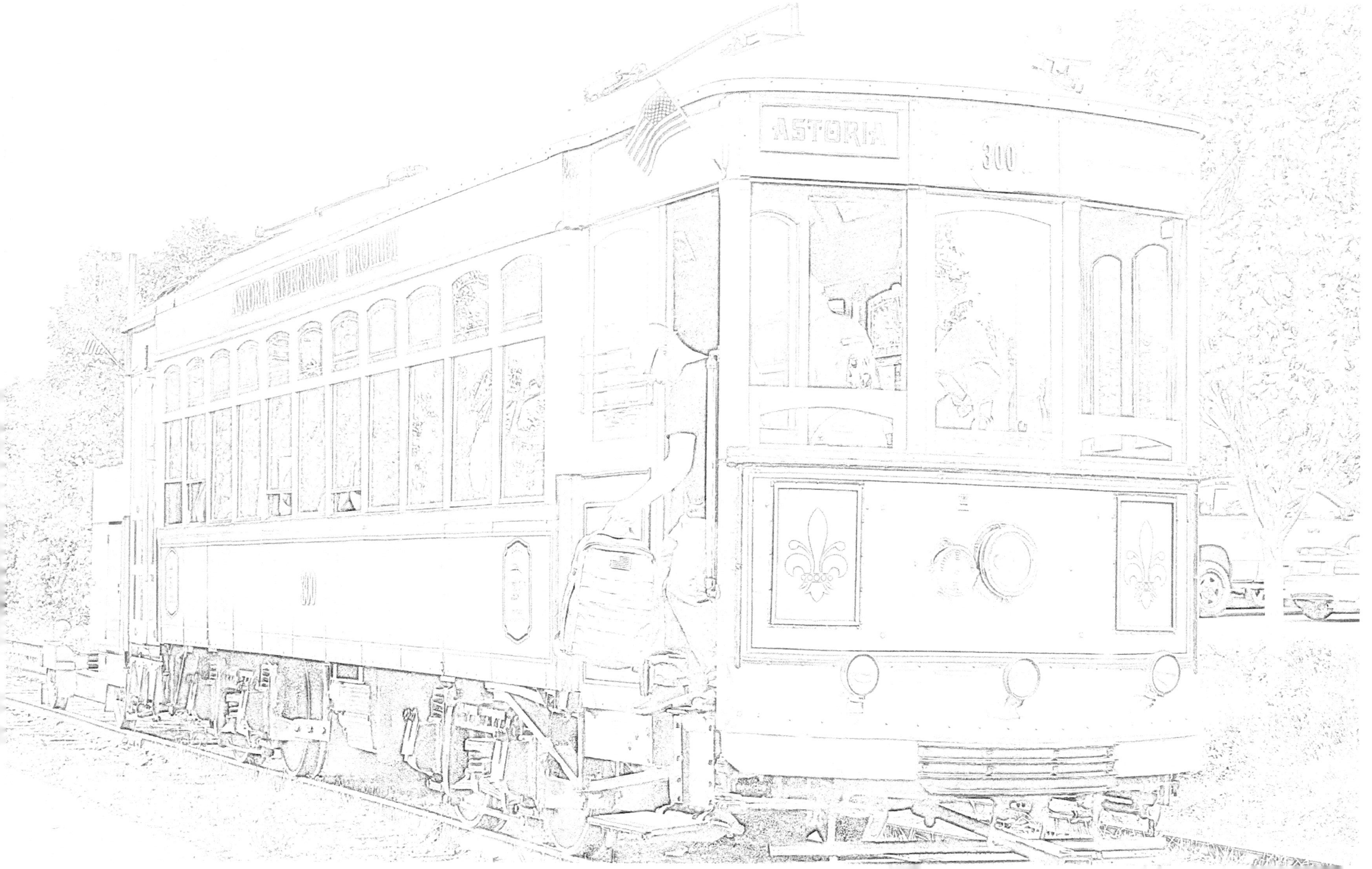
ASTORIA
300
ASTORIA RIVERFRONT TROLLEY

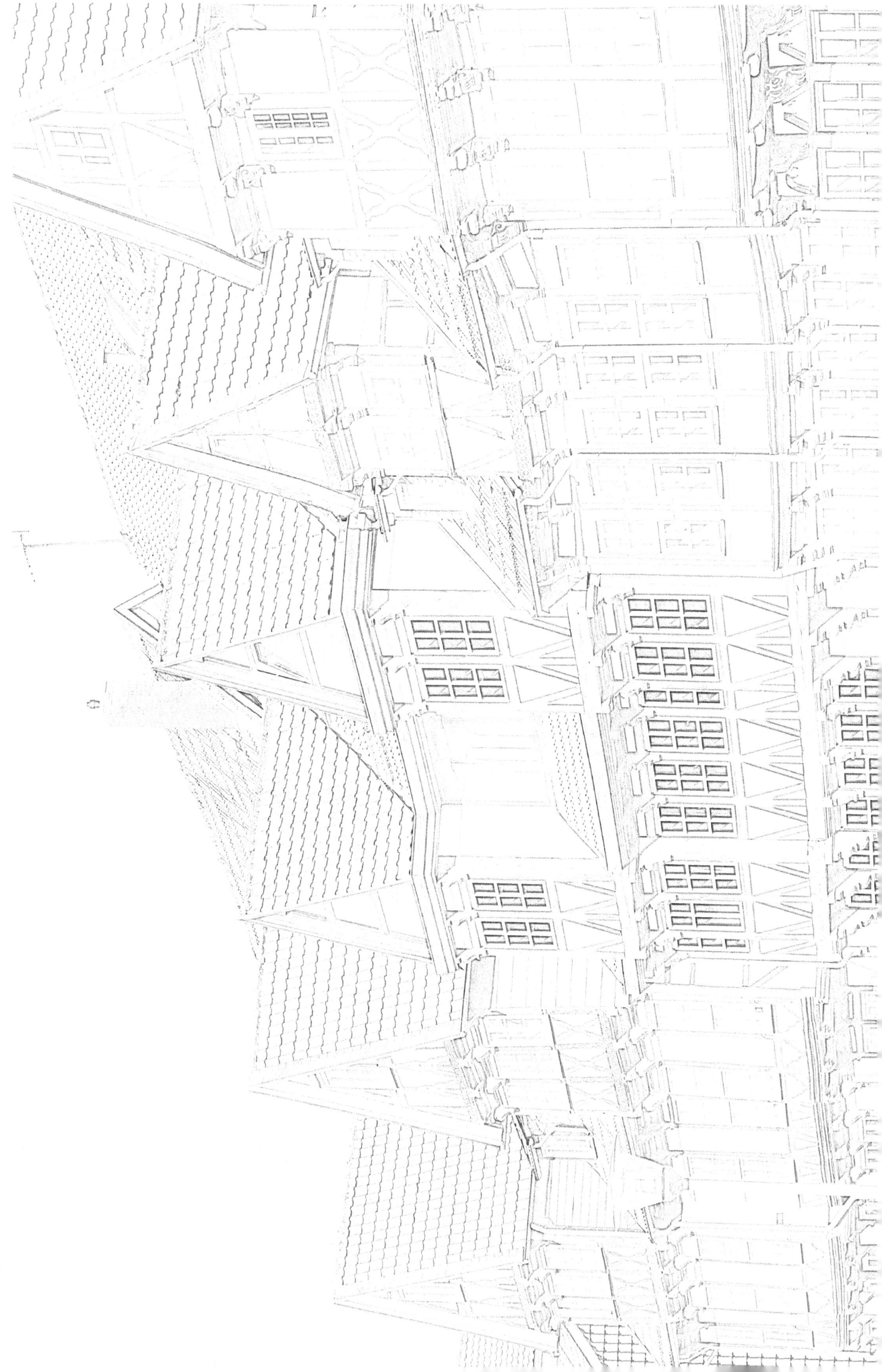

مصنع تيتي
للالباستر
ALABASTER craftsm
-TITI-ARABI-

www.ingramcontent.com/pod-product-compliance
Lightning Source LLC
Chambersburg PA
CBHW081056180526
45170CB00005B/1784
* 9 7 8 0 3 5 9 8 6 4 7 8 2 *